Differentiating the Curriculum

Supporting Teachers to Thrive in Mixed-Ability Classrooms

RALPH PIROZZO

Acknowledgements

The author is grateful to Pip Riordan and Ros Mangold for their permission to include their unit titled 'The Very Hungry Caterpillar' and the associated Learning Centres in this book.

© 2024 Ralph Pirozzo

This work is copyright. Apart from any pages identified as reproducible and any fair dealings for the purposes of private study, research, criticism or review, or as permitted under the Copyright Act, no part should be reproduced, transmitted, stored, communicated or recorded by any process, without written permission. Any pages identified as reproducible are only authorised for use in the classroom or by any school or nonprofit organisation that has purchased the book. Enquiries should be made to the publisher.

Published in 2024 by Amba Press, Melbourne, Australia.
www.ambapress.com.au

First published in 2013 by Hawker Brownlow Education.
This edition replaces all previous editions.

ISBN: 9781923215061 (pbk)
ISBN: 9781923215078 (ebk)

A catalogue record for this book is available from the National Library of Australia.

Contents

Introduction 1

Chapter 1: Ability Grouping 27

Chapter 2: Cooperative Learning Teams 35

Chapter 3: Learning Contracts 47

Chapter 4: Learning Centres 61

Chapter 5: Multi-age Grouping 85

Chapter 6: Individual Learning Plans 103

Chapter 7: Concluding Remarks and Summary 123

Appendix 1 131

Appendix 2 132

Figures

Please note that all figures are available in full colour as downloadable resources. Visit go.hbe.com.au and enter the password provided in the imprint page.

Introduction

    Figure 1: Differentiating and Individualising the Curriculum:
    The Pirozzo model 2

    Figure 2: Year 7 Reading Results 4

    Figure 3: Year 7 Mathematics Results 4

    Figure 4: Gathering Information for Differentiation 7

    Figure 5: The Learning & Teaching Wheel 10

    Figure 6: Percentage of Time Devoted to LOTS and HOTS 11

    Figure 7: The Thinking Classroom Level 3 12

    Figure 8a: Bloom's Taxonomy 1 of 3 13

    Figure 8b: Bloom's Taxonomy 2 of 3 13

    Figure 8c: Bloom's Taxonomy 3 of 3 14

    Figure 9: The Engaging Wheel 15

Figure 10: Ralph's Area of Maximum Potential 17
Figure 11: Summary of Research on Bloom's Taxonomy
and Multiple Intelligences 18
Figure 12: The 48 Grid Planning Matrix 19
Figure 13: The 56 Grid Planning Matrix 19
Figure 14: The 56 Grid Planning Matrix:
Why Learn about Plants? (sample) 20
Figure 15: The 48 Grid Planning Matrix: Saving the Koala (sample) 21
Figure 16: 10 Steps to Creating Outstanding Units 23

Chapter 1: Ability Grouping

Figure 17: The 48 Grid Planning Matrix: Countries of the World 29
Figure 18: Countries of the World: Ability Grouping 31–32

Chapter 2: Cooperative Learning Teams

Figure 19: Cooperative Learning Roles 38
Figure 20: LDC (Likes, Dislikes, Challenges/Changes) 39
Figure 21: The 56 Grid Planning Matrix:
Build a Space Station in Outer Space 41–43

Chapter 3: Learning Contracts

Figure 22: The 48 Grid Planning Matrix – Why Learn about Plants? 51
Figure 23: Learning Contracts (Based on a Total of 50 Points) 52
Figure 24: Learning Contract: Why Learn about Plants? 53
Figure 25: Learning Contract: Rubric 55
Figure 26: Learning Contract: Progressive Assessment Grid 56

Chapter 4: Learning Centres

Figure 27: The 56 Grid Planning Matrix: The Very Hungry Caterpillar 70
Figure 28: Learning Centre 1 71
Figure 29: Learning Centre 2 72
Figure 30: Learning Centre 3 73
Figure 31a: Learning Centre 4a 74
Figure 31b: Learning Centre 4b 74
Figure 31c: Learning Centre 4c 75
Figure 31d: Learning Centre 4d 75
Figure 32: Learning Centre 5 76
Figure 33: The 48 Grid Planning Matrix:
Marketing Your Boat (Year 9) 78–79

Figure 34: Activity 8 80
Figure 35: Activity 25 80
Figure 36: Activity 27 81
Figure 37: Activity 28 81
Figure 38: RAT 82
Figure 39: Activity 58 82
Figure 40: Activity 59 83

Chapter 5: Multi-age Grouping
Figure 41: The 56 Grid Planning Matrix: Keeping Healthy 97–99

Chapter 6: Individual Learning Plans
Figure 42: LD, EAL/D and Disadvantaged Students:
Individual Learning Plan (Jeff) 112–113
Figure 43: The Average Student:
Individual Learning Plan (Melissa) 114–115
Figure 44: The Gifted and Talented Student:
Individual Learning Plan (Cheryl) 116–117
Figure 45: The Student with Challenging Behaviour:
Individual Learning Plan (Pat) 118–119

Concluding Remarks and Summary
Figure 46: Summary of Learning and Teaching Strategies 129

Introduction

Teachers who are effectively using differentiation in their classroom will understand that while they cannot change the school's content descriptors, success for all students relies on a flexible delivery of the curriculum.

Differentiation is recognising that in mixed-ability classes, students can have very different:

- abilities
- learning styles
- backgrounds
- prior knowledge
- interests
- experiences
- willingness to learn

Maker (1982) and Tomlinson (1999) have emphasised that teachers can differentiate the curriculum by altering the content, process, products and the learning environment. The underlying philosophy of this book is that, in addition to altering these factors, teachers need to implement a variety of powerful learning and teaching strategies in order to effectively differentiate the curriculum.

The purpose of this book is not to review and/or critique the work of these highly regarded models, however, it does take for granted that teachers are aware of them. In the event that some teachers have not yet read the work of Maker and Tomlinson, then we believe that they should do this at their earliest opportunity.

I am committed to the view that, while teachers may not always be able to change the content as prescribed by the relevant syllabi (particularly in high schools), they have an enormous control in the way they present or package this content for their students. They can choose from six different learning and teaching strategies to deliver this content, as indicated in the Pirozzo Model (see page 2).

The Pirozzo Model heavily relies on the teacher's willingness to adopt a multi-level delivery system in order to maximise every students' learning potential. By using the teaching and learning strategies presented in this book, teachers will provide students with various approaches to:

- learning the prescribed content using their preferred learning styles
- choosing their preferred pathway to create their Real Assessment Tasks (RATs)
- demonstrating what they have learnt in a variety of exciting and engaging ways
- developing the skills to work in cooperation with their peers or by themselves
- reflecting and evaluating on how they learn, how they retain learnt information and how they retrieve this knowledge when needed

Differentiating and Individualising the Curriculum
The Pirozzo Model

THE MATRIX
The Learning and Teaching Wheel and The Engaging Wheel

| Ability Grouping | Cooperative Learning Teams | Learning Contracts | Learning Centres | Multi-age Grouping | Individual Learning Plans |

Figure 1

Similarly, when teachers accommodate for students' diverse thinking skills and learning styles, this fosters the attitude needed to create a classroom environment that promotes differentiation, reflection and innovation.

This book offers step-by-step instructions on how to effectively implement the six approaches in the classroom, as shown in the Pirozzo Model (see Figure 1). I strongly believe that these six effective teaching and learning strategies should be available to all students in every classroom, giving the learner the opportunity to choose the activities that will be most valuable to them. Teachers should be *proactive* rather than *reactive* to the demands of the differentiated classroom, meaning students will have more than one strategy available, enabling them to complete their assigned Real Assessment Tasks (RATs). In a fully differentiated classroom, the 'one size fits all' approach will not suffice.

In 1978 while I was head of remedial education at a large secondary school, I commenced two longitudinal studies that set out to prove the necessity of differentiating a mixed-ability classroom. As an integral part of this school's enrolment policy, every student is assessed in reading and mathematics during their last year of primary school.

A large number of reading tests are available to assess students' reading abilities, such as Gapadol, NEALE, PAT-R, Raven's Progressive Matrices, TORCH and Waddington. The Gapadol Reading Comprehension Test (McLeod & Anderson 1972) was chosen for this study because it is easy to administer, and provides the researcher with a student's reading age in years and months. Then, by comparing their reading age with their chronological age, we can obtain an objective measurement of the students' progress in reading (Pirozzo 1982a; Pirozzo 1982b).

The original study was based on a sample of 1004 students and indicated that, although the students' average reading age was relative to their chronological age (C.A. 12.6; R.A. 12.15), this hid a distribution of reading abilities from seven years to over 16 years and ten months (see Figure 2). Within this distribution, 23.6 per cent of the students were identified as severely disadvantaged readers, whereas 6.4 per cent were identified as superior readers. This data also indicated that boys outnumbered girls about 3:1 in the severely disadvantaged reading group, whereas girls outnumbered boys by about 3:1 in the superior reading group (Pirozzo 1983).

To ascertain students' ability in mathematics, the Promoting Learning International Mathematics Diagnostic Test (devised in 1978 and published in 2012) was used. To date, this test has been administered to over 10 000 Year 6 and 7 students. This test contains a total of 42 multiple choice questions that attempt to review the work covered in maths at a Year 6 and 7 level.

The results (see Figure 3) indicated a very wide spread of correct answers, ranging from 7 to 42. Since the original study was conducted, over 10 000 students have been tested with the Promoting Learning International Mathematics Diagnostic Test, with the average score being 28 out of 42 with a standard deviation of five. Based on these results, it would appear that students achieving a score below 23 will encounter severe difficulty with high-school mathematics, thus requiring a great deal of assistance. Students obtaining a score higher than 33 will need extension work.

Differentiating the curriculum: Supporting teachers to thrive in mixed-ability classrooms

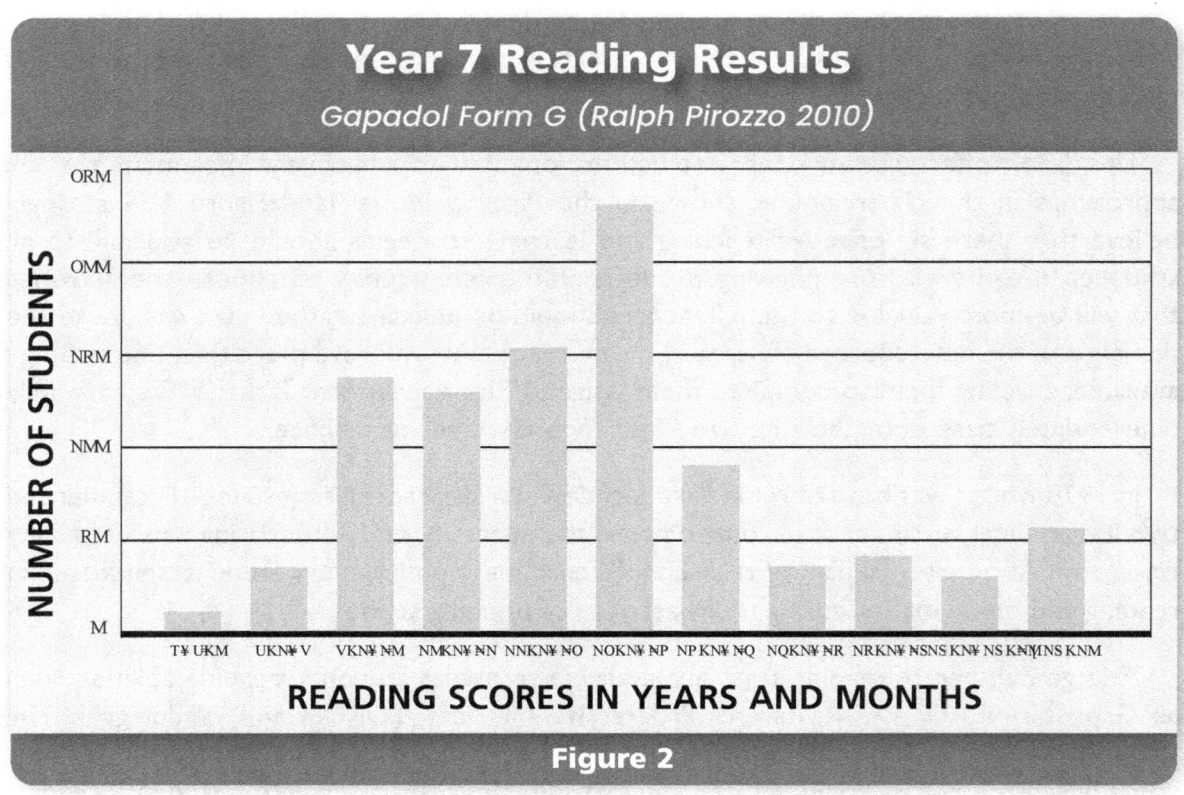

Figure 2

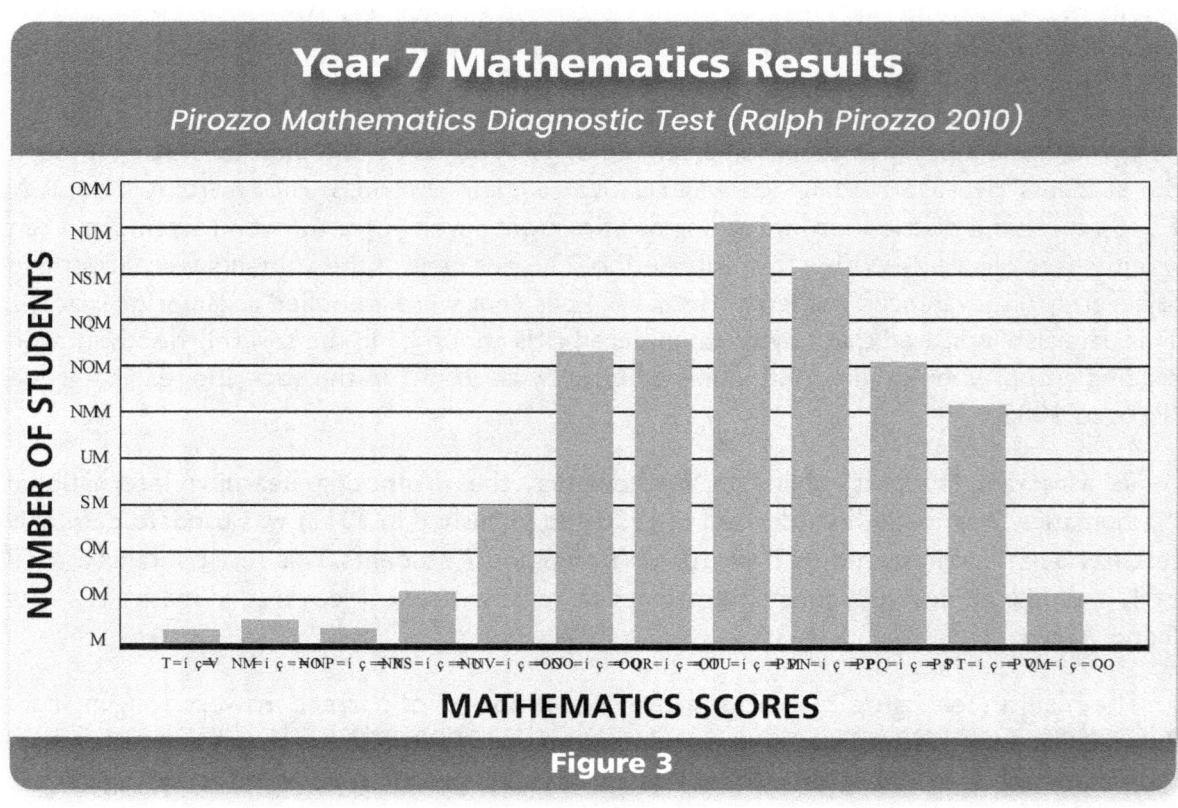

Figure 3

Of major concern to teachers is the fact that we have used this test since 1979, and while the average score has remained relatively constant at 28 out of 42, the standard deviation has steadily increased, indicating that the spread of abilities in our classrooms is getting bigger rather than smaller. This will pose major challenges to teachers of mixed-ability classes.

Assumptions and cautions

In the original study, a number of important factors needed to be considered in interpreting these results. Firstly, it is possible that a number of students received low scores on the Gapadol Reading Comprehension Test, not because they lack an innate ability, but because they may not be conversant with the language used in the test. Secondly, in view of the fact that Promoting Learning International's Mathematics Diagnostic Test relies heavily on reading ability, it is conceivable that students with reading disabilities will inevitably do poorly on this test (Pirozzo 1983).

The data emanating from working with thousands of teachers in Australia, Canada, China, New Zealand, Singapore and the UK and that of my two longitudinal studies indicates that in any mixed-ability classroom, students will display a huge range of abilities in all subject areas. For example, more recently Goddard and Howarth (pers. comm 2012) reported that their F–2 students displayed:

- reading ages from 5–10 years
- spelling ages from 5–10.5 years
- PM Levels from 2–22

Furthermore, data released in Australia by the 2013 NAPLAN (National Assessment Program for Literacy and Numeracy) Summary Report indicates that in numeracy, reading, writing, spelling, grammar and punctuation, students' achievements at Year 3, 5, 6 and 9 differ greatly between schools, states and territories. This is shown by the number of students working above, at or below the national minimum standards in each year level.

This huge range of abilities can be found in any mixed-ability class, with major implications for the way teachers deliver the curriculum. Fundamentally, the data tells us that in any mixed-ability classroom we will have at least three groups of students, namely:

- students with learning difficulties
- average learners
- gifted and talented students

This means that if the teacher were to 'teach to the middle', inevitably students with learning difficulties would feel completely lost, while the gifted and talented students would be bored. According to Goddard and Howarth's multi-age classroom, one could not possibly teach to the middle. In fact, where is the middle in this F–2 classroom? Does it mean that the teacher aims their teaching at the Year 1 level? If this were to be the case, one can only imagine what would happen to the children at Foundation level and to the Year 2 students in this classroom.

Given this wide range of abilities and learning styles, differentiation is a must if teachers are going to thrive in mixed-ability classrooms. Students need a classroom that provides them with the most exciting and challenging learning environment, where they will be exposed to both explicit teaching and choice in which activities they undertake. It's important that their thinking skills and learning styles are acknowledged and nurtured through a variety of different learning and teaching strategies.

Based on extensive work with over 20 000 teachers, I believe that to fully differentiate the curriculum, teachers need (1) an in-depth knowledge of their students, and (2) a strong planning framework that enables teachers to engage their students through a combination of explicit teaching and choices.

1. Gain an in-depth knowledge of your students

We are unlikely to meet the specific learning needs of students unless we know a great deal about them. This can be done by administering a variety of tests, both formal and informal. The obtained data should include students' reading ages, mathematics scores, preferred levels of thinking and their preferred learning styles and interests.

Formal Data Gathering

- Reading tests such as: Gapadol, NEALE, PAT-R, Raven's Progressive Matrices, TORCH and Waddington
- Mathematics Diagnostic Test by Promoting Learning International
- Improving Thinking: Multiple Intelligences Test by Hawker Brownlow
- My Preferred Levels of Thinking Test by Promoting Learning International
- Checking students' records

Informal Data Gathering

- A variety of inventories or informal class discussions and interviews
- Discussions with other teachers, year-level coordinators, head of departments, principals, deputy principals and guidance officers
- Meetings with parents, guardians, grandparents and social workers

This information can be gathered and tabulated on the 'Gathering Information for Differentiation' form (see Figure 4).

I have been fortunate enough to work with many teachers who are prepared to devote a good deal of their time and energy in gathering information about their students. In this very important phase, they ask the support of specialist teachers (such as enrichment teachers and guidance officers) who carry out the relevant tests on their behalf.

These teachers do this because experience has taught them that you cannot differentiate the curriculum without having extensive knowledge of your students.

Gathering Information for Differentiation
(Ralph Pirozzo 2013)

Information required to differentiate and individualise the curriculum

STUDENT: _____ YEAR LEVEL/STAGE: _____ TEACHER: _____

D.O.B.	C.A.	R.A.	TEST RESULTS					COMMENTS		
			Gapadol	Neale	Raven	TORCH	Other tests	RAMP (R. Pirozzo 2007)	Teachers	HODs/ DPs/ Principals	Guidance Officer

Additional comments from parents/guardians/grandparents/police/social workers/welfare officers
_____
_____

Figure 4

2. A strong planning framework that enables teachers to engage their students through a combination of explicit teaching and choices

In 1985, when I was the head of science at a very large comprehensive high school, I commenced my search for a planning framework that would give teachers the opportunity to engage students through explicit teaching, while still providing them with choices. I was frustrated by some of my students' lack of interest in the subject matter being taught, poor academic results and significant discipline problems resulting in huge amount of time devoted to 'putting out little fires'. By inviting my peers to observe my lessons and provide feedback, I quickly realised that my classroom was:

- teacher-centred and content-driven
- teaching to the middle
- dominated by students copying notes from the blackboard (there were no IWBs back then)
- driven by asking plenty of low-level thinking questions
- poorly structured with students sitting in rows
- poorly decorated with no posters on the walls
- absent of any choice whatsoever to the students

It was obvious that this delivery mode wasn't working, so I decided to start improving my practice by reviewing the relevant literature. In doing this I created a list of 53 theories and 10 taxonomies to study. In the early 1990s, while I was a regional consultant for gifted and talented students, I worked alongside teachers from both primary and secondary school. During this time, it was discovered that:

- the use of Bloom's Taxonomy is extremely effective when working with students of different abilities
- the concept of multiple intelligences was found to be particularly valuable when working with students who have different learning styles

In an attempt to summarise my research, Bloom's Taxonomy was found to be extremely useful in providing a well-defined thinking framework. At the lower-order levels – Knowing, (known by some researchers as Remembering), Understanding and Applying – students are required to provide clearly-defined answers to show how they can solve a problem based on what they already know and understand. We refer to these levels as Lower Order Thinking Skills (LOTS). Here, students may be asked to write the first draft of their story, solve maths problems and carry out simple chemical experiments.

At the higher-order levels – Analysing, Creating and Evaluating – students are encouraged to apply critical thinking processes, thus developing their Higher Order Thinking Skills (HOTS). For example, at the analysing level students should be able to break knowledge into its parts. This means having students deconstruct the draft of their story with the assistance of their teachers and/or peers, exploring how their maths knowledge can be used in the community (e.g. who actually uses their knowledge of 'perimeter') and identifying the critical variables in their science experiments.

At the Creating level we are more interested in the students re-assembling these parts to create something new and unique. At the Evaluating level, we want our students to be able to discuss and assess their opinions, decisions and recommendations. In other words, can they justify:

- why they have made the relevant changes to their stories
- how Pythagoras' Theorem can be utilised with words, images and symbols
- why the science experiment they conducted works, or doesn't work, and are able to determine the variables that may impact on its success. In other words, can the student elaborate?

In 2004, we saw the need for the addition of a sub-level to Bloom's Taxonomy was identified, leading to the introduction of Pre-Knowing. This level was added specifically to cater to the needs of children with learning difficulties, EAL/D (English as an Additional Language or Dialect) students, disadvantaged learners, very young children and refugees.

The question remains of how teachers can help their students to move from using LOTS to using HOTS in a meaningful and structured manner. The following material may prove useful:

- The Learning and Teaching Wheel (or, The Thinking Classroom – Level 1)
- The Thinking Classroom – Level 2
- The Thinking Classroom – Level 3
- Bloom's Taxonomy: Sample questions and learning activities

Teachers can use The Learning and Teaching Wheel to engage their students by using:

- Seven levels of thinking
- 92 critical verbs
- 91 choices, based on Glasser's Choice Theory (1986)

In addition, teachers should use The Learning and Teaching Wheel (see Figure 5) while planning units, teaching lessons and assessing students' work using rubrics. There should be a total alignment between the rubrics used and The Learning and Teaching Wheel so that, from the very beginning, students know exactly what quality of work is required to achieve an A, B or C.

Fundamentally, the use of the 92 critical verbs (found in the ring of The Learning and Teaching Wheel) should permeate the classroom discourse to become an integral part of the classroom's culture, rather than students encountering them only during tests and exams. This is particularly relevant for students who come from environments where they are unlikely to be exposed to instructional verbs such as 'formulate', 'prioritise' and 'critique'.

Suppose that at the end of a test or exam, the teacher discovers that the students have done very well with the LOTS, but rather poorly on the HOTS. The teacher has a

The Learning & Teaching Wheel

Devised by Ralph Pirozzo (2005) based on Bloom's Taxonomy (1956)

LOTS — Lower-Order Thinking Skills

Left outer list:
- Definitions
- Diagrams
- Dictionary
- Events
- Films
- Magazines
- Models
- Newspapers
- Radio programs
- Readings
- Tape recordings
- TV shows
- Websites

Top segment terms: Collages, Analogies, Conclusions, Diagrams, Drawings, Drama, Graphs, Outlines, Photographs, Posters, Skits, Statements, Speeches, Stories, Summaries, Translations

Right outer list:
- Calculations
- Cartoons
- Collections
- Diaries
- Dioramas
- Drama
- Emails
- Films
- Illustrations
- Models
- Paintings
- Photographs
- Projects
- Web pages
- Websites

Inner wheel — Knowing: Copy, Find, Name, Know, Relate, List, Remember, Listen, State, Locate, Write, Tell, Trace, Look

Understanding: Describe, Comprehend, Explain, Understand, Convert, Express, Outline, Draw, Interpret, Restate, Match, Retell, Share, Translate

Applying: Apply, Calculate, Classify, Illustrate, Carry out, Use, Make, Complete, Play, Do, Show, Plan, Solve, Examine, Report, Prepare, Record

Analysing: Analyse, Survey, Categorise, Arrange, Distinguish, Identify, Compare, Contrast, Investigate, Separate, Organise, Examine, Deconstruct, Select

Creating: Compose, Estimate, Conduct, Create, Improve, Imagine, Propose, Predict, Devise, Plan, Formulate, Suggest, Construct, Perform, Design, Invent, Research

Evaluating: Argue, Rate, Advise, Debate, Assess, Determine, Decide, Evaluate, Verify, Discuss, Recommend, Justify, Critique, Prioritise, Review, Judge

Centre: **Pre-Knowing**

HOTS — Higher-Order Thinking Skills

Left outer list:
- Arguments
- Assessments
- Conclusions
- Debates
- Decisions
- Evaluations
- Judgments
- Musicals
- Paintings
- Recommendations
- Reviews
- Trials
- Web pages
- Websites

Bottom segment terms: Books, Games, Answers, Cartoons, Advertisements, Experiments, Articles, Plays, Reports, Magazines, Poems, Inventions, Models, Pantomimes, PowerPoint presentations, Products, Questions, Radio and TV programs, Recipes

Right outer list:
- Arguments
- Assumptions
- Charts
- Commercials
- Conclusions
- Diagrams
- Graphs
- Hypotheses
- Laws
- Questionnaires
- Reports
- Statements
- Surveys

Figure 5

tremendous opportunity to concentrate on the verbs located in the Analysing, Creating and Evaluating areas of the Learning and Teaching Wheel in order to bolster students' ability to use Higher Order Thinking Skills.

Based on our extensive work with over 1000 schools across Australia, we can say with confidence that if schools are serious about enhancing NAPLAN scores, they are unlikely to see significant improvement unless students are encouraged to use HOTS on a regular basis.

Percentage of time devoted to LOTS and HOTS
(Ralph Pirozzo, 2012)

The Learning and Teaching Wheel can be used to differentiate the curriculum for three groups of students:

Level of Thinking	Children with Learning Difficulties	Average Learners	Gifted & Talented Students
LOTs (Lower Order Thinking Skills)	70%	50%	30%
HOTs (Higher Order Thinking Skills)	30%	50%	70%

Figure 6

The percentage of time indicated in the figure above should be used as a guide only, and will change dramatically depending on the ability and readiness of the students. For example, one would expect the amount of time dedicated to LOTS to increase significantly if the teacher were to be teaching a group of refugee students who have just arrived in Australia with no formal knowledge of the English language.

In addition to using The Learning and Teaching Wheel, teachers can also use The Thinking Classroom – Level 2 to formulate questions relating to Knowing, Understanding, Applying, Analysing, Creating and Evaluating. Along with the other figures in this book, 'The Thinking Classroom – Level 2' can be found in the downloadable resources at go.hbe.com.au.

If teachers are interested in discovering which thinking tools they should be using at each of the six thinking levels, they should use The Thinking Classroom – Level 3 (see Figure 7). These thinking tools appear throughout the book, mostly in relation to the activities shown in the matrix. A full description of each of the thinking tools featured can be found in my last book, *The Thinking School: Implementing Thinking Skills Across the School* (Pirozzo 2013). A list of all the thinking tools mentioned in this book can be found in Appendix 1 (page 131), along with the page number you can find them in *The Thinking School*.

Differentiating the curriculum: Supporting teachers to thrive in mixed-ability classrooms

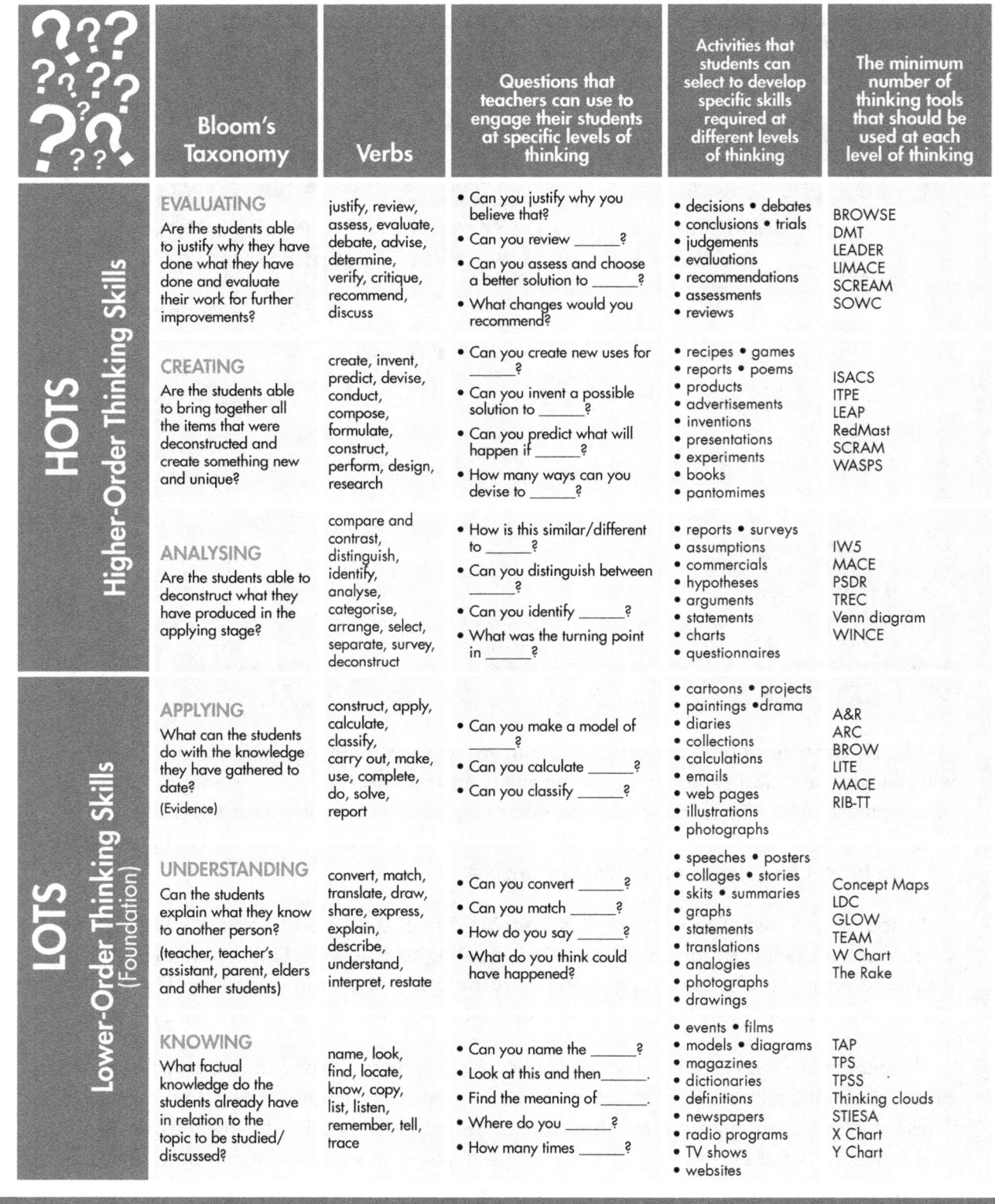

Figure 7

Please Note: In the event that the students had very little factual knowledge about the topic to be studied/discussed, the teacher should support them with 'concrete' material at the Pre-Knowing Level (The Pre-Knowing Level was added to Bloom's Taxonomy by Ralph Pirozzo in 2004).

By using any one of the Teaching Wheels presented so far, teachers have a minimum of 92 critical verbs relating to Bloom's Taxonomy at their disposal. Teachers can use these verbs to slowly scaffold their students from Knowing all the way to Evaluating. An example of how to do this is shown below.

BLOOM'S TAXONOMY: Sample Questions and Learning Activities (1 of 3)

THINKING LEVELS	USEFUL VERBS	SAMPLE QUESTIONS	LEARNING ACTIVITIES
KNOWING	Copy, Find, Know, List, Listen, Locate, Look, Name, Relate, Remember, State, Tell, Trace, Write	• Can you name the _____? • Look at this and then_____ • Find the meaning of_____ • How many times has _____? • What happened after_____? • What is the name of _____? • Who was the boy that _____? • Which is the right answer _____?	• List all the people in the story • Locate all the information that you can about the Second World War • Listen to your teacher • Look at the clock and tell me the time • Find the meaning of this word in the dictionary • Write the formula for photosynthesis • Name the capital of Canada • Copy the homework from the board • Trace this picture from the textbook • Remember what we learned yesterday • Tell your group what we need for this activity • State clearly what the soldier said in the story
UNDERSTANDING	Comprehend, Convert, Draw, Describe, Explain, Express, Interpret, Match, Outline, Restate, Retell, Share, Translate	• Can you write the formula for _____ in your own words? • Can you convert _____ to _____? • Can you give an example of a carnivore? • Can you write a brief outline of _____? • Can you match these two lists? • What do you think could have happened next in the story? • What was the main idea in _____? • Who do you think stole the _____? • Who was the main character? • How do you say _____ in French?	• Draw pictures to show how plants and animals interact together • Outline your plans for your next project • Explain the meaning of this symbol • Express how you feel in your own words • Draw a diagram/map/plan • Match these two lists • Retell the story in your own words. • Describe what the author meant by _____. • Restate this from the point of view of the villain • Share your drawings with your group • Translate this sentence from English into French

Figure 8a *(Ralph Pirozzo, 2006)*

BLOOM'S TAXONOMY: Sample Questions and Learning Activities (2 of 3)

THINKING LEVELS	USEFUL VERBS	SAMPLE QUESTIONS	LEARNING ACTIVITIES
APPLYING	Apply, Calculate, Classify, Carry out, Complete, Do, Examine, Illustrate, Make, Plan, Play, Prepare, Record, Report, Show, Solve, Use	• Can you calculate the number of tiles needed to cover this room? • Can you classify the following animals into the proper phyla? • Can you construct a rectangle with the following dimensions? • Can you plan and conduct an experiment? • From the information provided, can you _____? • Develop a set of instructions on how to operate _____? • Can you construct a model of _____?	• Show in a chart where all the plants are found in your suburb • Complete the following sentence • Construct a food chain using these animals • Classify the following organisms into their correct phyla • Illustrate the main ideas of the book • Make a clay model of a volcano • Calculate how many metres of wire are needed to fence the following paddock. • Solve the following math problems and show all your calculations • Examine this statement from the bully's point of view • Complete this flow chart showing the various stages of bread-making • Carry out this chemical experiment
ANALYSING	Analyse, Arrange, Categorise, Compare, Contrast, Distinguish, Examine, Identify, Investigate, Select, Separate, Survey	• Which events could not have happened? Why? • How is this similar/different? • How would the story have ended if _____ had happened? • Can you distinguish between _____? • What was the turning point in the play? • Can you explain what must have happened when _____? • Are there other possible outcomes? • Are there other motives behind _____? • Can you identify the robber?	• Compare and contrast Asian and African elephants • Identify the strengths of this commercial • Categorise these items into plastic and metal • Construct a graph to illustrate the following relationship • Survey your friends in terms of their eating habits • Arrange these numbers from the largest to the smallest • Investigate how this discovery can be used • Analyse a work of art in terms of form, colour and texture • Select the best music for this play • Investigate how we can reduce bullying • Separate oil from water

BLOOM'S TAXONOMY : Sample Questions and Learning Activities (3 of 3)

THINKING LEVELS	USEFUL VERBS	SAMPLE QUESTIONS	LEARNING ACTIVITIES
CREATING	Compose, Conduct, Construct, Create, Design, Devise, Estimate, Formulate, Imagine, Improve, Invent, Perform, Predict, Propose, Suggest, Research	• Can you create new uses for _____? • If you had access to all the necessary resources, how would you deal with _____? • Can you invent a possible solution to _____? • Can you develop a proposal which would _____? • How many ways can you devise to _____? • Can you propose how we could improve this experiment? • Can you predict what will happen if _____?	• Create a new product and plan a marketing campaign for it • Propose how you will improve _____? • Invent a machine to accomplish a special task • Design a cover for a magazine • Compose a rhythm or add new words to a well-known tune • Devise an experiment that will extract more iron from its ore • Construct a model of the DNA molecule • Predict what will happen when _____? • Suggest ways to improve _____ • Conduct a survey to gather information about teenage smoking • Research how we can reduce world poverty • Estimate the cost of this marketing campaign
EVALUATING	Advise, Argue, Assess, Debate, Decide, Determine, Discuss, Evaluate, Judge, Justify, Priorities, Rate, Recommend, Review, Verify	• How would you defend your position in relation to _____? • What do you think about _____? • Can you assess and choose a better solution to _____? • How would you have handled _____? • What changes would you recommend to _____? Why? • Do you believe that _____? • How would you feel if _____? • How effective are _____? • What is the most valuable _____?	• Justify why you have chosen this particular piece of music for your school play • Discuss factors that should be considered when buying toys for young children • Verify that this is in fact the right answer • Debate: Should Australia mine uranium? • Determine whether this novel is suitable primary students • Verify that this maths formula is correct • Evaluate the research on AIDS • Judge which is the best short story • Decide on a criteria to judge a speech • Review this book and rate it from one to 10 • Recommend new strategies to be adopted based on your SOWC analysis.

(Ralph Pirozzo, 2006)

Figure 8c

Adapted by Ralph Pirozzo (2001) with permission of the Department of Education, Employment and Training, Victoria.

By engaging students with HOTS, teachers can align their practices with the Australian Curriculum where one of the seven General Capabilities deals specifically with critical and creative thinking.

Reflecting on Bloom's Taxonomy

We have shown that Bloom's Taxonomy is great for nurturing students' thinking skills, however, in our research we found that it does not fully provide for students' different learning styles. If teachers were to use Bloom's Taxonomy as their only vehicle to deliver the curriculum, then I believe that there will a significant number of disengaged students. To solely use Bloom's Taxonomy may mean that the teacher may feel they are thriving while some students are wishing they were somewhere else. Inevitably these disengaged students begin to play up, forcing the teacher to spend time 'putting out little fires', rather than do what they love doing most: teaching.

A very powerful theory that enables teachers to engage students through their preferred learning styles is Howard Gardner's Multiple Intelligence Theory. In 1983, a new view of intelligence was proposed that is defined as 'the capacity to solve problems or to fashion products that are valued in one or more cultural setting' (Gardner & Hatch 1989).

Using both biological and cultural research, Gardner (1983) postulated that there are at least seven intelligences. In 1999 Gardner added the Naturalistic, to be classified as the eighth intelligence, and has since indicated the possibility of other intelligences such as the Existential.

The eight intelligences:

- Verbal-linguistic
- Logical-mathematical
- Visual-spatial
- Bodily-kinesthetic
- Musical-rhythmic
- Interpersonal-social
- Intrapersonal-intuitive
- Naturalist

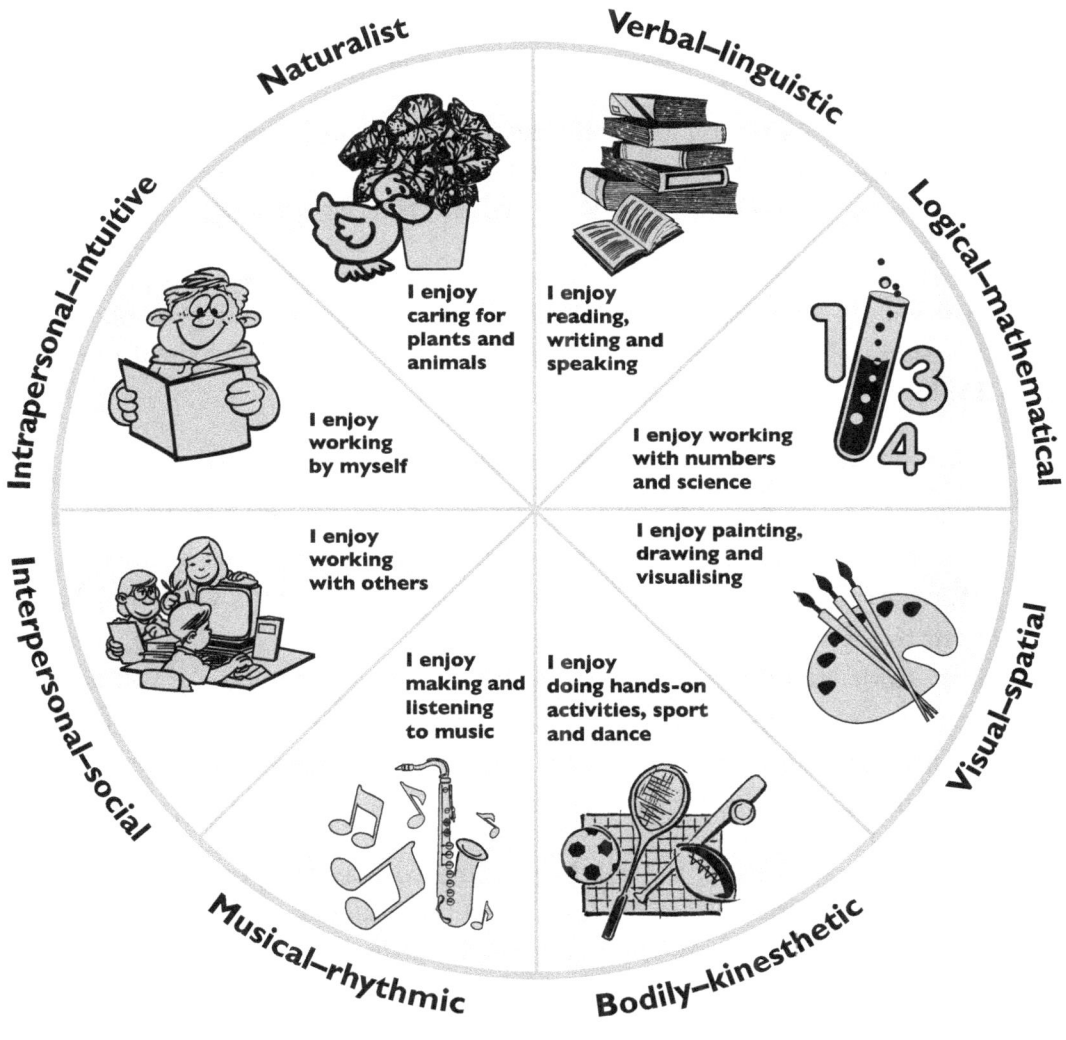

Figure 9

One of the key features of this theory is that it recognises that people can be smart in different ways. Undeniably, Multiple Intelligence Theory further supports the notion that each individual is unique. In the same way that we look different from one another, have different kinds of personalities and have our own gifts and talents, we also think differently. We all have different brains, which are wired differently.

Once we recognise that each student has their own unique set of intellectual strengths and weaknesses, teachers are in a position to structure the presentation of new material in a way that will engage different intelligences. If certain students learn best by talking and reasoning, looking and doing or cooperating and reflecting, teachers can use this information to fully engage these students.

One of the most remarkable features of Multiple Intelligence Theory is how it provides teachers with at least eight potential pathways to engage students. If a student is having difficulty learning some material through the linguistic or logical way of instruction, teachers have at least another six ways that they can present the material to facilitate learning.

A powerful way to introduce students to Multiple Intelligence Theory is to display a copy of The Engaging Wheel (Figure 9) in your classroom and to ask students to complete Hawker Brownlow's Multiple Intelligences Test (see page 134 for ordering details).

Once the students have completed this test, they should be provided with a copy of the RAMP (Ralph's Area of Maximum Potential) so they can list the three intelligences they scored highest in and place them in the Venn diagram (see Figure 10).

The students are now ready to colour in the centre of these overlapping circles. In so doing they will be highlighting their RAMP, that is their Area of Maximum Potential. The RAMP is similar but not identical, to Lev Vygotsky's Zone of Proximal Development (Wertsch 1985).

An excellent process that has been adopted by many teachers is to:

- display all the students' RAMPs around the classroom and encourage everyone to spend five minutes viewing the other students' work. Back in their regular seating arrangement, the teacher will then ask the students what they have learnt by viewing everyone's RAMPs.
- graph students' preferred learning styles, so that at a glance you will determine which students scored highest in each area. This information will be particularly useful when differentiating the curriculum, and will need to be stored in the students' portfolios for easy retrieval

Armed with this information, the teacher is able to maximise each student's learning potential by deliberately structuring the lessons so that students will be working about 50 per cent of the time within their RAMP. For example, let us suppose that the three multiple intelligences selected by a student were Visual-spatial, Bodily-kinaesthetic and Interpersonal-social. To get the best results for this student, the teacher will:

- provide the student with plenty of visual material such as posters, YouTube clips and content displayed on the IWB
- involve them in hands-on activities such as drawing, designing and constructing
- facilitate cooperative learning so they can work well with others

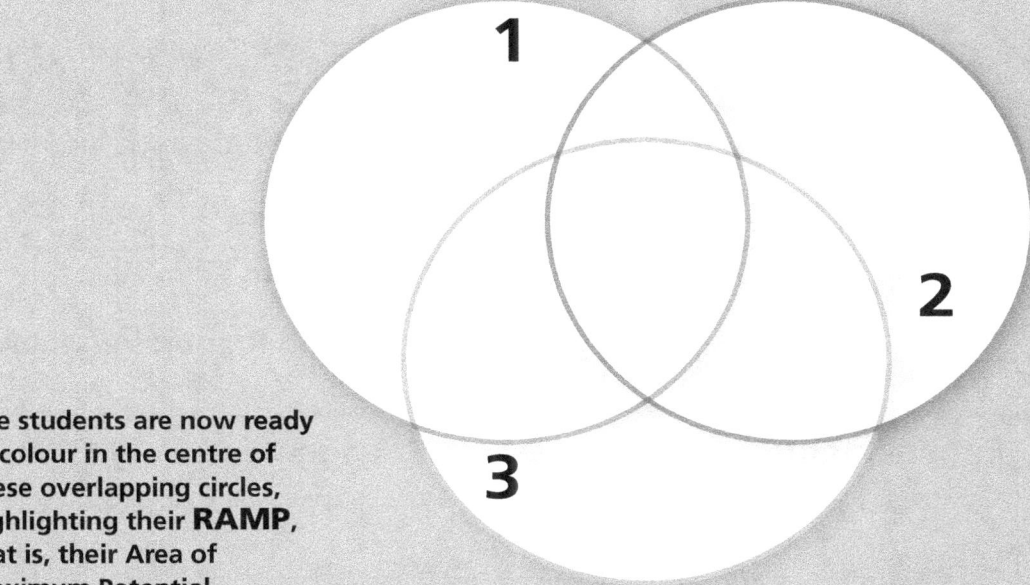

Figure 10

Reflecting on Howard Gardner's Multiple Intelligence Theory

While Multiple Intelligence Theory enables teachers to cater to students' preferred learning styles, it does not directly assist them to build depth and rigour in units, lessons and classroom activities.

For example, in many classrooms where the curriculum delivery model has been based solely on students' multiple intelligences we find that many students (including some of our brightest ones) will choose lower-level activities, thus becoming engaged in surface learning. In doing so these students produce 'fluffy' material that has very little depth and rigour.

Summary of the research on Bloom's Taxonomy and Multiple Intelligences

Since 1999 I've been advising schools not to use solely Bloom's Taxonomy or the Multiple Intelligence Theory. This is a result of classroom observations with thousands of teachers that commenced in 1985. My argument was based on the idea that, by using Bloom's Taxonomy, teachers provide for students' strongest thinking skills. By implementing Multiple Intelligence Theory, teachers engage students through their preferred learning styles.

I proceeded to ask myself, why not integrate these two outstanding models in order to take advantage of their strengths, while eliminating their limitations? Why not have the best of both worlds by designing a strong planning framework that would enable teachers to have both depth and rigour *and* engagement in their lessons? This is how, in 1997, the original 42 grid matrix was born.

Summary of Research on
Bloom's Taxonomy and Multiple Intelligences

Bloom's Taxonomy (1956)
when used in association with no other taxonomy and/or theory

Depth and Rigour: Very High

Engagement: Very Low
(particularly for low-achieving students)

Multiple Intelligences (1983)
when used in association with no other taxonomy and/or theory

Depth and Rigour: Very Low
(particularly for low-achieving students)

Engagement: Very High

Based on these findings, in 1997 Bloom's Taxonomy & Multiple Intelligences were integrated into a strong planning framework:

the matrix.

Fundamentally, the matrix enables teachers to simultaneously provide for students' thinking skills and preferred learning styles

Figure 11

Two years later, after Gardner's addition of the eighth intelligence, it was subsequently updated to the 48 grid matrix. Following the addition of a new sub-level in Bloom's Taxonomy called Pre-Knowing, the matrix was updated to a 56 grid in 2004.

It should be pointed out that while I was creating the matrix, other workers like Tony Ryan and Eric Frangenheim were also developing their own planning frameworks.

Using the 48 or 56 grid matrix

The matrix enables teachers to nurture their students' thinking skills while simultaneously engaging them through their preferred learning styles. A blank copy of both matrices are available below.

48 Grid Planning Matrix

Unit of study: Year Level:

Multiple Intelligences	Bloom's Taxonomy: Thinking Levels					
	Knowing	Understanding	Applying	Analysing	Creating	Evaluating
VERBAL — I enjoy reading, writing and speaking						
MATHEMATICAL — I enjoy working with numbers and science						
VISUAL/SPATIAL — I enjoy painting, drawing and visualising						
KINAESTHETIC — I enjoy doing hands-on activities, sports and dance						
MUSICAL — I enjoy making and listening to music						
INTERPERSONAL — I enjoy working with others						
INTRAPERSONAL — I enjoy working by myself						
NATURALIST — I enjoy caring for plants and animals						

Content descriptions/learning outcomes/the essential learnings:

Figure 12

56 Grid Planning Matrix

Unit of study: Year Level:

Multiple Intelligences	Bloom's Taxonomy: Thinking Levels						
	Pre-Knowing	Knowing	Understanding	Applying	Analysing	Creating	Evaluating
VERBAL — I enjoy reading, writing and speaking							
MATHEMATICAL — I enjoy working with numbers and science							
VISUAL/SPATIAL — I enjoy painting, drawing and visualising							
KINAESTHETIC — I enjoy doing hands-on activities, sports and dance							
MUSICAL — I enjoy making and listening to music							
INTERPERSONAL — I enjoy working with others							
INTRAPERSONAL — I enjoy working by myself							
NATURALIST — I enjoy caring for plants and animals							

Content descriptions/learning outcomes/the essential learnings:

(These matrices were devised by Ralph Pirozzo in 1997 & updated in 2004)

Figure 13

In the sample units we have adopted three colours: Please note that while these appear in grayscale in this book, they are available in full colour as downloadable resources.

- Blue (dark grey in book) – Explicit teaching. These activities will be taught to all students.
- White – Students can choose which of these they'd like to complete, either by themselves or in cooperation with other students. These provide the basis for differentiation, and are derived from the Glasser model.
- Yellow (light grey) – The tasks that the teacher will use for assessment and reporting purposes. These are Real Assessment Tasks (RATs), and should be located in the HOTS area. RATs require students to solve real-world problems, and were developed because a growing number of students found that much of what they learn at school was irrelevant to their lives.

Two sample matrices have been provided as a guide.

The 56 Grid Planning Matrix – Why Learn about Plants?

Year Level: EAL/D, F–2 and Children with Learning Difficulties

Multiple Intelligences	Bloom's Taxonomy: Thinking Levels						
	Pre-Knowing	Knowing	Understanding	Applying	Analysing	Creating	Evaluating
VERBAL I enjoy reading, writing and speaking	**Types of Plants:** trees bush grass flowers shrubs	Name the parts of a plant.	Explain how plants grow.	Read a book about trees.	Analyse the book about trees. What did you like the most about this book? Why?	**Real Assessment Task 1** Read *The Enormous Turnip*, then create your own narrative.	Read your narrative in front of the class and receive their feedback using the **LDC**.
MATHEMATICAL I enjoy working with numbers and science	**Verbs:** be chop cover cut die dig eat grow have plant put water	List all the known plants.	How many species of plants are there?	Examine the things that plants need in order to survive.	Discover how your plant grows.	Keep a record of your plant growth.	Evaluate the growth of your plant every week.
VISUAL/SPATIAL I enjoy painting, drawing and visualising		Bring your favourite plant to class.	Draw your own plant.	Label the parts of your plant.	Compare the plants in your country with the plants that are found in Australia.	Design a **Venn Diagram** using the information that you already have.	Are the plants found in your country different to the ones found in Australia?
KINAESTHETIC I enjoy doing hands-on activities, sports and dance		Participate in an excursion to the botanical gardens or local park. **Y Chart**	Describe the different kind of plants that you saw during the excursion.	Walk around the school grounds and look at the plants.	Compare and contrast the plants in your school grounds with those that you saw during the excursion. **Venn Diagram**	**Real Assessment Task 2** Create a box where you will be able to grow a small plant.	Evaluate the process of making your own box. How could you improve it? **TAP**
MUSICAL I enjoy making and listening to music	**Prepositions:** in/on under/above beside between **Thinking Tools** Teacher introduces the students to the following thinking tools from *The Thinking School* (2013) prior to using them in the appropriate context: LDC TAP Y Chart X Chart PSDR TPS LEAP Venn Diagram	Listen to songs about plants, forests and/or the environment.	Explain the meaning of your chosen song to your group.	Sing this song in English (for EAL/D students)	Using various instruments, begin to compose your own song or dance.	Create your own song or dance. **LEAP**	Present this song or dance to your class. **LDC**
INTERPERSONAL I enjoy working with others		What did you like most about the excursion to the local gardens?	Share your thoughts with a partner. **TPS**	In your group, discuss the things that plants need to grow.	What would have happened if your plant did not receive any light? **PSDR**	**Real Assessment Task 3** Devise an experiment that will show what happens when plants do not receive any light.	How could you have improved your experiment? Share your suggestion with the class.
INTRAPERSONAL I enjoy working by myself		Read simple worksheets about plants.	Complete simple worksheets about plants.	Match the words to the pictures.	Using the **Y** or **X Chart**, share with your team how you feel when a tree is cut down?	Create a dictionary of plants (in English and in your own language).	Using your dictionary, teach another student what you have learned about plants.
NATURALIST I enjoy caring for plants and animals		List the parts of a plant: branch trunk flower fruit leaf petals roots seeds stem	Explain why plants need: light soil sun water	Examine why these animals are associated with plants: ant bee beetle spider butterfly ladybird grasshopper	Categorise the animals that are associated with plants.	Plant your favourite vegetable in the school garden.	What could you do to improve growing your vegetables? Advise your group or class.

Content descriptions/learning outcomes/the essential learnings:

Figure 14

The 48 Grid Planning Matrix – Saving the Koala

Year Level: 8

Multiple Intelligences	Bloom's Taxonomy: Thinking Levels					
	Knowing	Understanding	Applying	Analysing	Creating	Evaluating
VERBAL I enjoy reading, writing and speaking	2. Carry out a **Thinking cloud** and then list all the endangered species.	7. Explain why the whale has not become extinct.	19. Use the **BROW** strategy to prepare a TV/newspaper/ radio ad to protect the koala.	18. Why should we prevent other species from becoming extinct?	**Real Assessment Task** How will you prevent the koala from becoming extinct? Your action plan will be presented to various groups including students, teachers, administrators, parents, local government officials and a number of environmental experts	
MATHEMATICAL I enjoy working with numbers and science	4. Visit www.savethekoala.com to find out how many koalas we have at present.	9. Use **TREC** to find out how much it will cost to prevent the koala from becoming extinct. In your estimate, include cost associated with buying land, materials and labour.	23. Use the **TAP** strategy to brainstorm all the things that you can do to prevent the koala from becoming extinct.	24. Now, categorise the things that you can actually do to prevent the koala's extinction.		
VISUAL/SPATIAL I enjoy painting, drawing and visualising	1. Look at posters and photographs of extinct animals that your teacher brought to class.	5. Visit www.savethekoala.com. Then, draw a map to show where most koalas live.	16. Make a timeline of when dinosaurs were alive. Why did they become extinct?	25. Create a **Venn diagram** of koalas versus whales. What do they have in common?	41. Create your own web page about saving the koala. Present it to your group and receive their feedback. You may choose the **LDC** tool as an evaluation strategy.	
KINAESTHETIC I enjoy doing hands-on activities, sports and dance	10. Participate in a field trip to the local koala sanctuary and/ or visit your local park.	13. Make cut-outs of your favourite endangered species.	17. Role play your favourite endangered species using a **W Chart**. Why have you selected this one?	20. Organise a poster/chart/ collage for your favourite endangered species.	34. Create and perform a play dealing with tree clearing.	36. Devise an environmental game that could be used to teach others. **WASPS**
MUSICAL I enjoy making and listening to music	11. Learn a song about saving an endangered species.	14. Choose a song about people caring for the environment and explain its meaning to your group.	42. Choose the music to be played while presenting your action plan.	21. Arrange the music to be played while presenting your action plan.	26. Compose a rap/jingle/song to save the koala. **LEAP**	37. Act and choreograph a dance about saving the koala's habitat.
INTERPERSONAL I enjoy working with others	29. What can your group do to stop a species from becoming extinct? **TAP**	6. When is an animal endangered? Discuss this with your group.	33. Interview the manager of your local zoo to discover how they keep koalas alive.	31. Use **The Rake** to design a model of the best environment for the koala to live in. Ensure that its habitat has plenty of space for climbing, feeding, breeding and sleeping.	32. Present your ideas for the best environment for the koala to live in to your class. **LDC**	
INTRAPERSONAL I enjoy working by myself	8. Should we keep animals in zoos? What is your opinion?	22. Visualise yourself as an endangered species. How do you feel? Now, complete a **Y Chart**.	15. Imagine a day in the life of a young koala. Now, write a story to be published in the school newsletter and/or the local paper. **BROW**	27. Share with your group your concerns about tree clearing. Identify how this can be stopped. Who can help you to achieve this?	38. You are standing in front of a koala while its "habitat" is being destroyed. Now complete an **X Chart**.	40. Assess whether the koala will be extinct by the year 2020 by using the **SOWC Analysis**.
NATURALIST I enjoy caring for plants and animals	3. What would your life be without plants and animals? **TPSS**	12. How do you feel when you see a koala that has been rescued from a car accident on TV?	28. How would you promote the idea of preserving an endangered species?	35. Analyse the things that you can do to become more environmentally friendly.	30. Review the book *Where the Forest Meets the Sea*. Imagine you are the child in the book **Y Chart**	39. Determine the impact of tree removal on the survival of the koala.

Content descriptions/learning outcomes/the essential learnings:

Figure 15

You will see here that by using the matrix, students know from the very beginning exactly what they have to do to achieve As, Bs or Cs, and how their teachers are going to help to get them there.

You will notice that in the 'Saving the Koala' units there is a number next to each activity. These numbers indicate the teacher's scope and sequence, that is, the way the unit will be taught. One would expect that for students to create their RATs, the teacher would have a clear idea on how the activities should be sequenced for maximum impact. The numbering of the activities is based on Bruner's Spiral Curriculum (1966). This means commencing the lesson by building a strong foundation, and every layer enables the teacher to add another layer on top of the previous layer, and so on. Bruner reminds us to ensure that students have mastered the prerequisite knowledge and skills before new information is introduced.

In order to achieve depth, rigour and engagement in our classroom, we encourage teachers to follow a very detailed and precise planning process (see Figure 16).

Units planning can be commenced by identifying the relevant content descriptors – this is nothing new. What *is* new and exciting is that traditionally, we would now proceed to teach this unit without due regard to what students would be expected to do in order to demonstrate the relevant content descriptors.

Based on the work of McTighe and Wiggins (2004) we have added two additional steps to the planning process. By applying the theory of Backward Design we see to it that once the relevant content descriptors have been identified, we no longer rush to our classrooms to teach the unit. Instead, we now devote a good deal of time and energy in brainstorming and deciding:

1. What do we want our students to be able to do at the end of the unit that will enable them to demonstrate the relevant content descriptors?
2. How will we know whether students' work has depth and rigour, while meeting the criteria set for receiving As, Bs and Cs? A different rubric will need to be generated for each RAT.

Some teachers I work with find the idea of having to state the expected outcomes for students at the beginning of the planning cycle rather daunting. The best thing we can do is to actually plan a unit with them to show that this is not the case.

When it comes to unit planning, I often use the example of building a new house or renovating an existing one. We would expect the builder to draw up the relevant plans to show us exactly what the house will look like upon completion. We would want to know where the kitchen, bedrooms and toilets are located. Having signed the contract, the builder then proceeds to 'work backward' – that is, they'd use a bobcat to excavate the site. After the excavation has been completed, the concrete is poured over the steel girders to make sure that the foundation is solid and from there on the bricklayers, carpenters, tile layers and painters work to build the house based on the specifications as set out in the brief. The builder's brief is similar to our RAT.

We wouldn't think very highly of a builder who would say that they have no idea what the house would look like once finished, and that we will have to wait and see where the kitchen, bedrooms and toilets are going to be located.

As teachers, we do not build or renovate houses, but we do build curriculum plans that have depth, rigour and engagement. This is critical if we are to ensure that every student in our care is provided with the most engaging, exciting and challenging learning environment.

10 Steps to Creating Outstanding Units

1. Clearly identify the content descriptors from the relevant syllabi.

2. a) Create Real Assessment Tasks (RATs) that the students need to complete in order to demonstrate the relevant content descriptors.

b) Develop a rubric for each RAT. This rubric will be used for teaching and assessment purposes. Colour the RAT yellow.

3. a) Select your critical verbs from The Learning and Teaching Wheel (based on Bloom's Taxonomy). The Learning and Teaching Wheel will provide you with 92 critical verbs.

b) Use a variety of questions so that your students will develop both Lower Order Thinking Skills (LOTS) and Higher Order Thinking Skills (HOTS).

4. Determine your students' preferred Multiple Intelligences, thereby providing for eight different learning styles.

5. a) Decide what you will be teaching (explicit teaching) and what choices you will provide to your students.

b) Colour the explicit teaching blue and leave the choices white.

c) State how you will differentiate the curriculum using at least six different learning and teaching strategies.

6. Hyperlink a minimum of five different thinking tools in your unit.

7. Engage your students with a number of Cooperative Learning Activities.

8. Show how you will deliver your unit in a logical and sequenced manner by assigning a number to each activity in the sequence in which you will teach this unit.

9. List the appropriate resources needed to teach this unit.

10. Align your unit to the new Australian Curriculum.

Figure 16

Summary

In order to fully provide for the thinking skills and learning styles of students in mixed-ability classes, differentiation is key. For this to happen, teachers need to have an in-depth knowledge of their students and a strong planning framework that enables them to engage their students through a combination of explicit teaching and choices.

Teachers can gain an in-depth knowledge of their students by administering a variety of formal tests, and also through informal means such as inventories and talking to teachers, principals and parents.

For a strong planning framework, teachers can use the matrix. This multi-level framework derives its strength from Bloom's Taxonomy (1956) and its flexibility from Multiple Intelligence Theory (1983). More recently, the work of McTighe and Wiggins (Backward Design), Bruner (Spiral Curriculum), Glasser (Choice Theory) and Vygotsky (Zone of Proximal Development) have been fashioned on the matrix in order to make it more responsive to student learning. Since its inception in 1997, the matrix has enabled primary and secondary teachers to provide for students' thinking skills, while simultaneously engaging them through their preferred style of learning.

The matrix is used in this book for differentiation purposes because it provides teachers with a very strong and highly-flexible foundation on which to layer a variety of effective learning and teaching strategies. In fact, the rest of this book will detail how units based on the matrix enable teachers to differentiate the curriculum by implementing the Pirozzo Model. The underlying philosophy of the Pirozzo Model is that teachers will implement a minimum of six learning and teaching strategies in their classrooms to differentiate the curriculum. These strategies are:

- Ability Grouping
- Cooperative Learning Teams
- Learning Contracts
- Learning Centres
- Multi-age Grouping
- Individual Learning Plans

Each learning and teaching strategy will be dealt with as a separate section of this book.

References

Bloom, B S, ed., 1956, *Taxonomy of Educational Objectives*, Longman, London.

Bruner, J 1966, *Toward a Theory of Instruction*, Harvard University Press, Cambridge, MA.

Gardner, H 1983, *Frames of Mind*, Fontana Press, London.

Gardner, H & Hatch T 1989, 'Multiple intelligences go to school: Educational implications of the theory of multiple intelligences', *Educational Researcher*, vol, 18, no, 8, pp. 4–10.

Gardner, H 1999, *Intelligences Reframed: Multiple Intelligences for the 21st Century*, Basic Books, New York, NY.

Glasser, W 1986, *Control Theory in the Classroom*, Harper & Row, New York, NY.

Maker, C J 1982, *Curriculum development for the gifted*, Pro-Ed, Austin, TX.

McLeod, J & Anderson JJ 1972, *Gapadol Reading Comprehension Test*, Heinemann, Melbourne, Victoria.

McTighe, J & Wiggins G 2004, *Understanding by Design*, Association for Supervision and Curriculum Development, Alexandria, VA.

Pirozzo, R 1982a, 'Bridging the gap between low reading ability and high text difficulty in the secondary school', *Australian Journal of Reading*, vol. 5, no. 4, pp. 192–201.

Pirozzo, R 1982b, 'Making sense of textbooks', *Education News*, vol. 17, no. 11, pp. 10–14.

Pirozzo, R 1983, 'The range of reading and mathematical ability displayed by first year high school students', *The Educational Administrator*, vol. 20, pp. 37–41.

Pirozzo, R 2007, *Improving Thinking in the Classroom,* 2nd edn, Hawker Brownlow Education, Melbourne, Victoria.

Pirozzo, R 2013, *The Thinking School: Implementing Thinking Skills Across the School,* Hawker Brownlow Education, Melbourne, Victoria.

Tomlinson, C 1999, 'Leadership for differentiated classrooms', *The School Administrator*, vol. 9, no. 56, pp. 6–11.

Wertsch, JV 1985, *Vygotsky and The Social Formation of Mind*, Harvard University Press, Cambridge, MA.

Chapter 1
Ability Grouping

Ability Grouping, tracking or streaming emerged as an organisational response due to the differences in students' cultural and social backgrounds, academic abilities and maturity.

As pointed out by Hopkins (2006), logic, emotion and research often clash in the long standing debate over the advantages and disadvantages of Ability Grouping, Tracking or Streaming. These types of groups continue to be a contentious issue in education. A central question is whether Ability Grouping leads to high achievement for all, or whether it unfairly limits the educational opportunities for disadvantaged students, thereby exacerbating existing educational and social inequalities (Nomi 2010).

The question still remains as to whether or not Ability Grouping is an efficient way to handle differences in student abilities. Does such grouping benefit students or does it unfairly label them?

Ability Grouping should not be confused with tracking or streaming. Usually, Ability Groups are small, informal groups formed within a single classroom. Assignment to a certain Ability Group is often determined by the classroom teacher, and is always:

- short-term, never lasting more than one school year
- varied by subject
- kept off the students' records

On the other hand, tracking or streaming differ from Ability Grouping in scale and permanence. Being assigned to a certain tracking is often determined by the principal, deputy principal or head of department, and is:

- long-term, lasting at least two school years
- the same for all subjects
- recorded in the students' records

I am opposed to using tracking or streaming on the basis that this extreme form of grouping does not improve students' achievement and can create a toxic learning environment for both students and teachers. I remember being given four classes of low ability students in my first year as a teacher in Australia. At this comprehensive high school, students were streamed based on a subjective perception of ability and placed in classes such as Year 8(17), 9B3, 9C3 and 10B7. Imagine walking into a classroom full of 36 low-achieving Year 9 boys or 36 low-achieving Year 9 girls and try to teach them all about the structure of the atom on a Friday afternoon in 36-degree heat with no fans or air conditioning!

Unfortunately for low-achieving students, tracking leads them and their teachers to take on unflattering labels, often resulting in low expectation, accompanied by appalling behaviour. How often I would hear our 36 low-achieving Year 9 boys justifying their poor behaviour by saying, "What do you expect from us, we're the 9B3 boys!"

In a comprehensive review of research on different types of Ability Grouping, Slavin (1986) found that grouping students as a class by ability for all subjects doesn't improve their achievement. Furthermore, in her book *Crossing the Tracks: How Untracking Can Save America's Schools*, Wheelock (1992) argues that once students are grouped, they generally stay with the same group for their entire school career and their levels of low achievement become exaggerated over time. More recently, Clarke and Clarke (2008) emphasised that generally, only very high achieving students may benefit from setting up ability classes in mathematics, with a negative impact on average and low-attaining students. They point out that once ability classes have been established:

- they can lead to mistaken perception that individual differences are no longer an issue
- many schools assign their least-qualified teachers to low ability classes
- teachers of low ability classes often have low expectations of what students can do
- students are often grouped in accordance with narrow criteria and it is assumed that these classes are appropriate for all kinds of tasks and content areas
- despite claims of flexibility, lower ability classes are very hard to leave
- ability classes cannot be supported in the interest of social justice

While opposing tracking or streaming, I favour Ability Grouping – that is, grouping students heterogeneously for most of the school day – I regroup them according to ability for one of two subjects. Groups may be set up within a class for a specific amount of time to help students who are having difficulty with specific skills or to extend gifted students.

By looking at the Year 5 geography unit based on the matrix titled 'Countries of the World' (Figure 17), we can easily discover what will be taught to the students – these are represented by the activities in the blue squares (dark grey in the book). We can also see what activities the students can choose, as these are represented by the activities in the white squares. The yellow activities (light grey in book) show what the teacher expects the students to complete as part of their Real Assessment Tasks.

Note: In the following figures, "CC" refers to the students' chosen country.

Chapter 1 - Ability Grouping

The 48 Grid Planning Matrix - Countries of the World
Year Level: 5

Bloom's Taxonomy: Thinking Levels

Multiple Intelligences	Knowing	Understanding	Applying	Analysing	Creating	Evaluating
VERBAL I enjoy reading, writing and speaking	List the capital city of your chosen country (CC).	Explain why you have chosen this country. **TAP**	Prepare a short story/poem about your CC.	Analyse a book/story that has been published in your CC.	**Real Assessment Tasks** 1. Create a radio or TV ad.	Review and improve your CC's web page.
MATHEMATICAL I enjoy working with numbers and science	How much will it cost to live in your CC for a week/month/year?	How is your CC trading with the rest of the world?	Complete a map of your CC showing its major areas of industry and mining.	Investigate any damage done by your CC's industry and mining.	2. Design an effective marketing campaign for your CC.	Justify the amount your CC spends in promoting its industry and mining. Is it working?
VISUAL/SPATIAL I enjoy painting, drawing and visualising	Locate on a map, your CC's major cities.	Draw a world map showing where your CC is located.	Make a model of a typical farmhouse in your CC.	Compare and contrast your CC with Australia in terms of sports.	3. Construct a poster, collage or cartoon relating to your CC.	Using the SOWC Analysis, determine what your CC will be like in 2025.
KINAESTHETIC I enjoy doing hands-on activities, sports and dance	Name the five most important sports played in your CC.	Explain the rules of your CC's national game.	Demonstrate a game played by children in your CC to your group/class.	Organise and choreograph a dance about your CC.	4. Devise and perform a play about your CC.	Prepare and evaluate a recipe for one of your CC's known foods. **SCRAM**
MUSICAL I enjoy making and listening to music	Learn a song from your CC and sing it to the class.	Play a song from your CC on your favourite musical instrument.	Write a song, jingle or rap about your CC. **LEAP**	Perform your song, jingle or rap to your class and receive their feedback **LDC**	5. Based on your class' feedback, compose your final song, jingle or rap about your CC. **LEAP**	Perform your song, jingle or rap about your CC in front of your entire school and videotape it.
INTERPERSONAL I enjoy working with others	You have just arrived in your CC. Share your experiences. **Y Chart**	Share with your group the major issues facing young people in your CC. **TPS**	As a group, show how your CC could generate more jobs.	How would your life change if you were to move to your CC?	6. Conduct a mock interview with your CC's leader. **X Chart**	Evaluate how much your class knows about your CC. **Thinking clouds**
INTRAPERSONAL I enjoy working by myself	Why would you like to live in your CC?	What do you like the least about your CC?	Impersonate a well-known person living in your CC.	As your CC's new PM, what would you change? **TAP**	Complete a **Y Chart** on a child living in your CC.	Evaluate your life in your CC. Write an autobiography. **The Rake**.
NATURALIST I enjoy caring for plants and animals	List the major plants and animals that are found in your CC.	Are any of these plants and/or animals listed as endangered species?	Examine the impact made by tourists whilst visiting your CC. **The Rake**	Based on your analysis from the previous activity, create a map that tourists could use whilst visiting your CC. This map should aim to cause the least amount of damage to your CC's environment.		Prepare a marketing plan for your CC's tourism, based on the results of your SOWC analysis.

KEY: CC = Chosen Country

(This matrix was devised by Ralph Pirozzo in 1997 and updated in 2004)

Figure 17

Implementing Ability Grouping

A teacher working at a school in a small rural town has decided to depart from their normal delivery mode, and instead has chosen one of the six learning and teaching strategies that make up the Pirozzo Model. Below are the steps that will enable a teacher to easily adapt this unit into five different Ability Groups.

1. Decide on how many groups you would like to establish. The teacher of this unit has decided to set up five different Ability Groups that align with Bloom's Taxonomy:
   - Group 1 – Knowing
   - Group 2 – Understanding
   - Group 3 – Applying
   - Group 4 – Analysing
   - Group 5 – Creating and Evaluating

2. Select the number of questions that you would like the students to answer. On this occasion, the teacher has chosen five different questions for all the Ability Groups, with the exception of Group 5 where the students are provided with eight questions.

3. Peruse the original unit called 'Countries of the World' and adapt the questions that you would like students to answer at the different ability levels. This is one of the most valuable attributes of the matrix. If as a teacher you felt that the original questions were useful, pertinent and worthwhile, then why would you not use them as the basis for designing the five Ability Groups?

4. Form your groups based on reliable data, with particular emphasis being placed on the students' reading and mathematics scores. Once filled, this information can be found on the 'Gathering Information for Differentiation' form (see Figure 4 on page 7).

5. Elect to have all students commencing their studies by completing Group 1 before proceeding to Group 2, and so forth. Given the enormous range of ability in this classroom, the teacher may elect to have more academically able students to skip the lower levels and proceed directly to answer questions found in Group 3. Prior to enabling students to skip Group 1 and 2, it should be stressed that the teacher checks with the students to ensure they have an in-depth knowledge of the material covered in the two lower groups.

6. Create the relevant answers for the questions asked and rubrics for the tasks to be completed by the students. These will be essential in order to provide students with objective feedback, assessment and reporting.

Countries of the World: Ability Grouping

Group 1: Knowing

In relation to your Chosen Country (CC):
1. Name its capital city and locate it on a map
2. List its five most important sports
3. Listen to five well-known songs from your CC. Select one song and sing it to your class in their language.
4. You have just arrived in your CC. Use the **Y Chart** to share your experiences with your group or class.
5. List your CC's native plants and animals

Group 2: Understanding

In relation to your Chosen Country:
1. List five reasons why you have chosen this country. Use **TAP** for your brainstorming.
2. Outline how your CC is trading with the rest of the world. You will need to list five of its major trading partners, major exports and major imports. Use graphs whenever appropriate.
3. Draw a world map and highlight your CC.
4. Explain the rules of your CC's national game.
5. Share with your group the major issues facing young people, with particular emphasis on education, sports, hobbies and employment.

Group 3: Applying

In relation to your Chosen Country:
1. Prepare a short story, poem or letter about your CC.
2. Complete a map showing its major areas of industry, mining and tourism.
3. Demonstrate a game played in your CC using **WASPS**.
4. Write a song, jingle or rap about your CC by using **LEAP**.
5. Examine the impact made by tourists whilst visiting your CC using **The Rake**.

Countries of the World: Ability Grouping

Group 4: Analysing

In relation to your Chosen Country:

1. Analyse a book, poem, story or letter published in your CC. Who was the author and what other works has he/she produced? Is she/he known internationally?
2. Using a Venn diagram, compare and contrast your CC with Australia in terms of sports. Name five well-known athletes in both countries and the sports that they are famous for.
3. Organise and choreograph a dance about your CC.
4. You have just been elected Prime Minister of your CC. Investigate what you would change about your CC and provide justifications for your decisions.
5. Based on your analysis in your previous activity, create a map that tourists could use whilst visiting your CC. This map should be as environmentally friendly as possible.

Group 5: Creating and Evaluating

In relation to your Chosen Country:

1. Design a marketing campaign for your CC aimed at attracting more tourists.
2. Create a poster, collage, cartoon or PowerPoint presentation relating to your CC.
3. Using the **SOWC** analysis, determine what your CC will be like in 2020.
4. Prepare and evaluate a recipe for a food that your CC's is known for. Use **SCRAM** and encourage your group to provide you with their feedback based on **LDC**.
5. Compose a song, jingle or rap about your CC. Perform in front of your entire school and videotape it.
6. Conduct a mock interview with your CC's leader based on the **X Chart**.
7. Complete a **Y Chart** on an indigenous or handicapped child living in your CC. Is there any discrimination taking place in your CC in relation to these individuals? How would you verify this?
8. Evaluate your life in your CC by writing an autobiography titled 'A day in the life of ...'.

Figure 18

Reflection

The move from a traditional teaching mode to the implementation of five Ability Groups was extremely successful based on the following:

- The students received higher marks than when the teacher used a more traditional teaching mode.
- The amount of on-task behaviour increased significantly, so the teacher was able to concentrate on helping students in their learning, rather than devoting time to 'putting out little fires'.
- The students found the Learning and Teaching Wheel particularly useful in locating which level of learning they were working within.
- The students had access to a large number of thinking tools as shown in the various Ability Groups. These thinking tools were extremely valuable as they enabled the students to access the curriculum and to transfer their learning from LOTS to HOTS. For this to work, it is critical that the teacher introduces these thinking tools prior to the commencement of this unit. A detailed coverage of these thinking tools is provided in my book *The Thinking School: Implementing Thinking Skills Across the School* (Pirozzo 2013).
- It should be emphasised that the aforementioned teacher was able to gain assistance with the monitoring of Ability Groups by a large number of parents. If this support wasn't available, the teacher will be stretched to properly support students with learning difficulties. Unless the teacher can rely on the support of parents or a teaching assistant, Ability Grouping may not be a suitable strategy for students with learning difficulties.

It is imperative that teachers who oppose Ability Grouping on philosophical grounds should not be coerced to adopt this teaching style. Instead, they should be encouraged to explore other learning and teaching strategies such as Cooperative Teams, Learning Contracts, Learning Centres, Multi-age Grouping and Individual Learning Plans.

References

Clarke, D & Clarke, B 2008, 'Is time up for ability grouping?', *Curriculum Leadership Journal,* vol. 6, no. 5.

Hopkins, G 2006. 'Is ability grouping the way to go—Or should it go away?', *Education World.* http://www.educationworld.com/a_admin/admin/admin009.shtml.

Nomi, T 2010, 'The effects of within-class ability grouping on academic achievement in early elementary years' *Journal of Research on Educational Effectiveness,* vol. 3, no. 1, pp. 56–92.

Pirozzo, R 2013, *The Thinking School: Implementing Thinking Skills Across the School,* Hawker Brownlow Education, Melbourne, Victoria.

Slavin, RE 1986, *Ability grouping and student achievements in elementary schools: A best-evidence synthesis,* Center for Research on Elementary and Middle Schools, Baltimore, MD.

Wheelock, A 1992, *Crossing the Tracks: How Untracking Can Save American Schools,* New Press New York, NY.

Chapter 2
Cooperative Learning Teams

Cooperative Learning Teams are an effective teaching strategy in which students work cooperatively in small, mixed-ability teams to complete a common task. The tasks are structured to maximise the learning potential of each member of the team. Therefore, Cooperative Learning Teams are a great way for all teachers to differentiate the curriculum, and an excellent alternative for those who believe Ability Grouping to be elitist.

Research on cooperative learning dates back to 1937 when social theorists discovered that group work was more effective and efficient in quality, quantity and overall productivity than when working alone (Gilles & Adrian 2003). More recently, cooperative learning has been shown to produce superior results in academic achievement, thinking skills and self-esteem across a wide range of subject areas and age groups (Bossert 1988–1989; Cohen 1994; Slavin 1990). Alice Macpherson from Kwantlen University College (2000–2007) reported that 90–95 per cent of people that lose their jobs do so because they cannot get along with the people they work with.

Teachers who have not yet implemented Cooperative Learning Teams in their classrooms may want to know how a cooperative classroom differs from what they would consider to be a traditional classroom. Johnson, Johnson and Smith (1991) offered the following comparison:

Traditional classroom

- Teacher is the 'sage on the stage'
- Lessons are structured and delivered in a way that students compete with each other
- Students can work by themselves to get the best possible marks without worrying about how well the other students are doing
- Students strive to do better than the rest of the class
- Rewards are viewed as limited
- The success of the individual and the failures of others are celebrated, i.e. I swim, you sink; I sink, you swim

Cooperative classroom

- Teacher is the 'guide on the side'
- The classroom is structured in a way that students learn together in order to maximise their own and each other's learning
- Students work together to achieve shared goals
- All members of the group strive for each other's success
- Students work in small heterogeneous groups
- Rewards are viewed as unlimited
- Group successes are celebrated, i.e. we sink or swim together

Johnson, Johnson and Holubec (1992) identified five basic elements of cooperative learning:

1. **Positive interdependence** – Students assist, encourage and support each other's efforts to learn.

2. **Individual accountability** – The performance of the individual student is assessed and the results are given to both the group and the individual student.

3. **Interaction through reflection** – Asking questions such as: what did each member do that was helpful to the group, and what can each member do to make the group work better?

4. **Skilled interpersonal communication** – Students need skills in leadership, decision-making, trust-building, effective communication and conflict-management.

5. **Interdependence through structure** – Students believe that they cannot succeed unless the other members of the group succeed, and vice versa.

Similarly, Kagan (1994) identified the following elements needed for cooperative learning:

- positive interdependence
- individual accountability
- equal participation
- simultaneous interaction

Both positive interdependence and individual accountability are common to both lists of attributes of cooperative learning. This is because positive interdependence needs to be structured into the team's activities, making members responsible for each other's success and, that individual accountability is an expected outcome of cooperative learning.

Interdependence means having unity and solidarity in achieving a common goal. It is best described by the motto made famous by Alexandre Duma in The Three Musketeers, 'All for one and one for all'.

Unfortunately, not all students were born with the skills to work cooperatively. If we do not equip our students with these skills, cooperative groups have the potential to become very noisy and unproductive. So how do we ensure the productivity of Cooperative Learning Teams? This can be achieved by using a three-pronged approach, as shown below.

1. Adopt Tuckman's (1965) and Tuckman & Jensen's (1997) five-stage model

This model shows how teams progress, the behaviours required to carry out tasks and how to develop positive, interpersonal interactions.

Stage 1: Forming

During this stage, students are usually on their best behaviour and conflict is avoided, as they seek to be accepted by others. Serious issues are not dealt with, as students are preoccupied with routine such as team organisation, who does what, when to meet and so forth. At this stage, team members are very focused on themselves.

Stage 2: Storming

This stage is seen as necessary for the growth of the team. Now that different ideas are competing for consideration, the team has to decide how they are going to complete the assigned tasks, and how they will function independently while contributing to the success of the team.

This stage can be unpleasant and upsetting, particularly to students who are averse to conflict. Unless the students have developed patience and tolerance for each other, there is a good chance the team will fail, thus never progressing past this stage.

Stage 3: Norming

By the time the group has progressed to the Norming stage, guidelines have been agreed upon and the focus is on the task to be accomplished. Some team members have had to give up their own ideas and agree with others to make for a functional team. The danger is that some members may be so focused on preventing conflict that they are reluctant to deal with controversial issues.

Stage 4: Performing

The group is now functioning as unit, tasks are being completed, dissent is dealt with in a way that is acceptable to the team and the team members are competent and able to handle decision-making without a great deal of supervision.

Stage 5: Adjourning and Transforming

This fifth stage was added by Tuckman and Mary-Ann Jensen in 1997. Stage 5 is the de-briefing stage, when the various teams celebrate their successes and reflect on what went well, what could be done better next time and then prepare to join other teams.

2. Train our students so they will develop the skills to work well in Cooperative Learning Teams.

Students can be trained to work in teams by assigning specific roles, as shown in the figure below. They learn that in a cooperative learning team they may be assigned the role of either the encourager, gatherer, timekeeper or recorder/reporter.

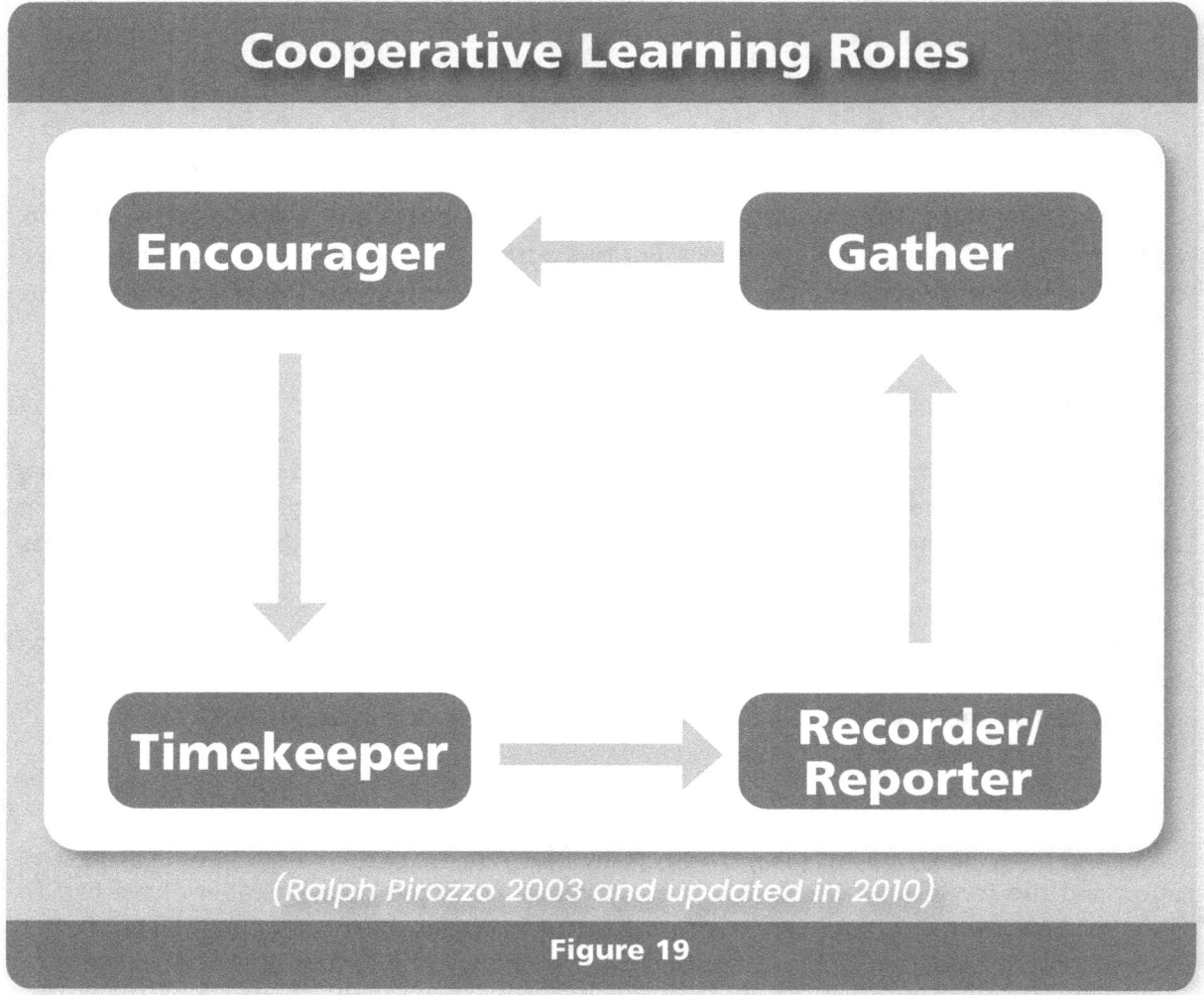

Figure 19

While students have an individual responsibility to carry out their designated roles, they have shared leadership to ensure that the group works well together. For example, once the gatherer has collected the materials needed for a particular activity, this doesn't mean that they can now do nothing until it's time to return the items to their original place. In the time between collecting and returning the relevant materials, the gatherer works with the other students to complete the assigned tasks.

In order to prevent students from being annoyed about carrying out the same role over and over again, designated roles should be rotated regularly. This will also give students the opportunity to develop the skills needed to perform all roles.

3. Assist students to develop the skills to provide effective feedback.

I've found the Likes, Dislike, Challenging/Changes (LDC) strategy to be particularly useful in training students to provide constructive feedback.

Like

What did you like about the other students or group's work? No negative comments are to be accepted at this stage. As the students become more confident in working cooperatively and gain experience in providing feedback, then they will be invited to provide feedback at Level 2 and Level 3.

Dislike

What didn't you like about the other students' or groups' presentation? Students are only to provide feedback relating to the task itself, and not about the student.

Challenging/Changes

What did you find challenging about the other students' or group's presentation? How could they change or improve their presentation?

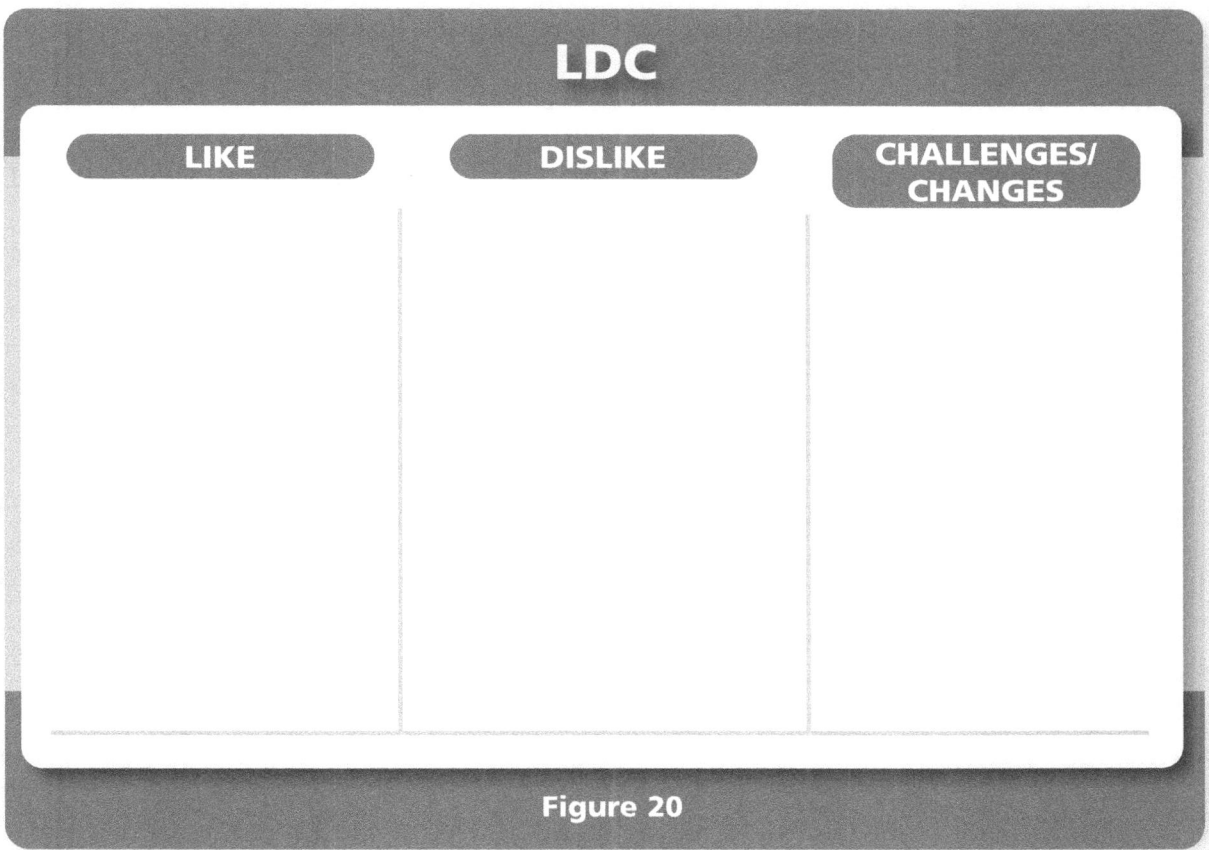

Figure 20

Implementing Cooperative Learning Teams

I implemented this theoretical data into the Cooperative Learning Teams strategy, as set out in the Year 6 unit 'Build a Space Station in Outer Space' (Figure 21). Given the fact that these students had already completed the Multiple Intelligences Test, it was decided to use the information contained in each student's RAMP (Ralph's Area of Maximum Potential) to form eight Cooperative Learning Teams. In addition, these students had previously received a good deal of training on how to work in Cooperative Learning Teams and how to provide effective feedback, therefore the teacher reviewed these skills at the commencement of the unit.

Characteristics of this Year 6 class

This class had 30 students, consisting of 16 boys and 14 girls. A total of eight groups were formed as follows: six groups with four students in each, and two groups with three students in each.

Each student had to work within their three preferred multiple intelligences. For example, if a student's RAMP indicated that their preferred multiple intelligences were (1) Visual, (2) Kinaesthetic and (3) Interpersonal then the expectation was that this student would join the Visual team, the Kinaesthetic team and the Interpersonal team respectively. This ensured that the students were placed in mixed-ability teams.

This unit lasted nine weeks and each cooperative learning team was expected to complete a minimum of three Real Assessment Tasks (RATs). This gave the students three weeks to complete each RAT. The students devoted 50 minutes per day to complete their RATs.

The 56 Grid Planning Matrix - Build a Space Station in Outer Space (1 of 3)

Year Level: 6

Bloom's Taxonomy: Thinking Levels

Multiple Intelligences	Pre-Knowing	Knowing	Understanding	Applying	Analysing	Creating	Evaluating
VERBAL I enjoy reading, writing and speaking (Team 1)	Teacher introduces unit to students. Teacher and students complete **Thinking clouds** on the question 'What are the attributes of an excellent report?' on the whiteboard/IWB. Teacher introduces/reviews **BROW, LITE** and **TAP**. Word Bank • comets • asteroids • planets • moons • gravity • space • solar system • eclipses • astronomy • Big Bang theory	Read notes from the following sources: • Young Astronomer • 100 Questions and Answers • Astronomy Today • The Collins Space Atlas www.kids-space.org www.nasa.gov www.space.com Teacher informs students that as an integral part of this unit, they will be expected to create a report, story, script, drama production, video or play relating to space exploration.	Define the following terms: • comets • asteroids • planets • moons • gravity • space • solar system • eclipses • astronomy • Big Bang theory Students, use the **Thinking clouds** to choose either a report, story, script, drama production, video or play. Teacher conferences with the students to ensure that they have the materials needed for their creation.	Should students choose to write a report, then they will use **BROW** to commence writing it. Make a rough draft of your report, story, script, drama production, video or play. Show your rough draft to your teacher and receive their feedback. **LITE**	Review your teacher's comments and make whatever changes are necessary.	**Real Assessment Task 1** Create your final report, story, script, drama production, video or play and receive feedback based on the relevant rubric.	Present your report, story, script, drama production, video or play to your class or school. Record your presentation on video. Use **TAP** to encourage your classmates to provide feedback.
MATHEMATICAL I enjoy working with numbers and science (Team 2)	Teacher revises basic understanding of place value, scales and measurement (e.g. mm, cm, m and km). Teacher introduces/reviews **TREC, PSDR** and **LEADER**.	Of what value is the sun to us? What determines eclipses, night and day? How does the earth's atmosphere provide for our needs (e.g. air)?	Why should we study the solar system or build space stations? Estimate how much it will cost to run a space station for a week. **TREC**	In building your station, how will you look after your workers in terms of: • clothing • food • sewage • oxygen • water • carbon dioxide • exercise • sleeping • social needs	Investigate how you will prevent the workers from suffering: • dizziness and nausea • muscle wastage • loss of calcium Select materials to take advantage of the sun's energy.	**Real Assessment Task 2** Assess your model and recommend changes so that it will work once in space. **PSDR**	Carry out a debate titled 'should space exploration continue?' **LEADER** Record your debate on video. Justify why you built your station in space.

Continued...

The 56 Grid Planning Matrix - Build a Space Station in Outer Space (2 of 3)

Year Level: 6

Bloom's Taxonomy: Thinking Levels

Multiple Intelligences	Pre-Knowing	Knowing	Understanding	Applying	Analysing	Creating	Evaluating
VISUAL/SPATIAL I enjoy painting, drawing and visualising (team 3)	Teacher introduces or reviews the Venn diagram.	Study various photographs of the Mir and other international Space Stations. View YouTube material relating to the Mir and international Space Stations. How will you help the workers to know where they are in the space station?	Draw a rough draft of your space station. Is it to scale? Will you paint the floors and ceiling in different colours? Why?	What colours have you chosen for the exterior and interior of the station? Show why you have chosen these colours? Now paint both the outside and inside of the station.	Compare one of the planets and space using a **Venn diagram**. Will this help explain why you have chosen to build your station in space?	**Real Assessment Task 3** Cooperate with the Kinaesthetic students to create the final model of your space station.	Makes suggestions on how your model can be improved. Review the colours that you have chosen and justify why you have chosen them.
KINAESTHETIC I enjoy doing hands-on activities, sports and dance (team 4)	Teacher revises cooperative learning strategies. Teacher explains that one Astronomical Unit (1 Au) = 149.6 million km. Earth = 1 Au Teacher introduces/reviews **WINCE** and **SCRAM**.	Look at a number of models of the solar system. Study photographs/videos of Mir and the International Space Station. What additional information will you need in order to build your own space station? **WINCE**	Explain what materials you will use in building your space station. Do you have experience in working with these materials? If not, what will you do to gain this experience? Will you be doing any science experiments? If the answer is yes, do you have the proper equipment?	Make a model of the solar system to scale. On your scale, use one Astronomical Unit (1Au) = 149.6 million km. This refers to the mean distance between the Earth and the sun. Prepare various tasty menus that will help your workers in reducing loss of calcium. Will the **W Chart** be of any value to you?	Select the materials that you will need to build your space station. On what basis will you be choosing these materials? Check with your teacher prior to assembling your model. Arrange various physical exercises that your workers can do to prevent muscle wastage.	**Real Assessment Task 4** Cooperate with students in the Visual group to create the final model of your space station. One member of your team has very high blood pressure. Use **SCRAM** to modify the meals for her/him. Identify the best exercise for one of the workers that has very poor blood circulation	How will you test your model to make sure that it will work? What criteria will you use? Have you asked your teacher to assist you in designing an appropriate rubric? See *rubistar.4teachers.org*.
MUSICAL I enjoy making and listening to music (team 5)	Teacher introduces or reviews **LEAP** and **LDC**.	Find and listen to songs that relate to space. View films and videos that relate to space research.	Describe to your group or class the meaning of one of these songs.	Examine songs, CDs and film clips that can be used to entertain the workers on the space station.	Arrange the music that will be available to your workers on the space station. **LEAP** Play it to your group and teacher and receive their feedback based on the **LDC**.	**Real Assessment Task 5** Based on your group, class or teacher's feedback, compose your final song, jingle or rap.	Play your song, jingle or rap to your class and evaluate how this music has been received by the other students. **LDC** Video your song, jingle or rap.

Continued...

Chapter 2 - Cooperative Learning Teams

The 56 Grid Planning Matrix - Build a Space Station in Outer Space (3 of 3)
Year Level: 6

Bloom's Taxonomy: Thinking Levels

Multiple Intelligences	Pre-Knowing	Knowing	Understanding	Applying	Analysing	Creating	Evaluating
INTERPERSONAL I enjoy working with others (Team 6)	Teacher introduces/reviews the **A&R, ARC, The Rake** and **TPSS**.	What traits do you have that will enable you to cope working in a close environment with others for months? Find out the maximum period of time that people can work in the space station. How big of an issue is weightlessness? How will your workers deal with it?	How will you select the workers needed on your space station? Write a job description for the space manager and have the other students in your group apply. Receive the applications, short list them and interview the applicants.	Use a concept map or the **Thinking clouds** to teach a younger student about the solar system. Was your concept map or **Thinking clouds** successful? How do you know? You may choose to use the **LDC** strategy to receive some feedback from the other students.	Choose the **A&R, ARC** or **The Rake** to solve conflicts that are likely to develop when individuals work in close areas.	**Real Assessment Task 6** Interview the manager of your space station. **X or Y Chart**	How successful was your interview? Did you ask the right questions? Were you fully prepared? Review how well you have worked as a group and make suggestions for improvements. **TPSS**
INTRAPERSONAL I enjoy working by myself (Team 7)	Teacher introduces or reviews the **X and Y Charts**.	How do you feel when you see astronauts working around the International Space Station on TV or YouTube?	Tomorrow you will be interviewed for the position of space station manager. Use **X or Y Chart** to prepare yourself for this interview.	Complete your own concept map or **Thinking clouds** to see how much you have learned about the solar system.	Investigate how space travel affects the human body. What can be done to prevent these problems?	**Real Assessment Task 7** Impersonate your favourite astronaut and answer questions. **X Chart**	Evaluate your life as the manager of the space station. Write an autobiography titled 'A day in the life of...'.
NATURALIST I enjoy caring for plants and animals (Team 8)	Teacher introduces or reviews the **SOWC** Analysis. Teacher revises the respiratory and cardiovascular systems and the process of photosynthesis.	Which plants are likely to survive and thrive in the space station?	Define **photosynthesis** and write a word formula for this process. What percentage of oxygen is in the air? What percentage of CO^2 is in the air?	Make a diagram of the stomata and explain how it works. How many litres of oxygen do you need per day? How much CO^2 do you produce per day?	Research the factors that increase the rate of photosynthesis. Research the factors that increase or decrease the amount of oxygen needed and the amount of CO^2 produced.	**Real Assessment Task 8** Estimate how many small plants are needed to produce enough oxygen to keep one person alive.	Is it likely that you can grow enough plants to satisfy the oxygen needed by the workers? Evaluate. Determine how your space station can operate in a way that will have the least impact on the environment. **SOWC**

Figure 21

Reflection

The implementation of eight Cooperative Learning Teams was extremely successful based on the following:

- The students received more As, Bs and Cs than when the teacher used a more traditional teaching mode. Furthermore, the level of creativity, willingness to attend school, enjoyment, motivation and self-esteem levels for most students greatly increased. However, three students did not work well in their respective Cooperative Learning Teams because they felt demeaned by having to work with students less academically able than themselves. These students could be described as gifted, and are usually very competitive and enjoy working by themselves.
- The incidence of discipline issues was extremely low, enabling the teacher to spend more time monitoring the various teams.
- Students found The Engaging Wheel particularly useful in discovering their preferred learning styles.
- The teacher taught the explicit teaching activities (the blue or dark grey activities in the Pre-Knowing column, which are dark grey in this book) to all students, regardless of which Cooperative Learning Team they belonged to – it was essential that all be exposed to this critical information. The teacher then devoted the rest of the time in monitoring the Cooperative Learning Teams, conferencing and co-constructing with the students and helping teams to prepare for their presentations.
- The activities in white squares indicate one pathway that the students could follow to complete their RATs. However, it was pointed out to the students that they can deviate from this path as long as they complete their RATs during the allocated time.
- The students had access to a large number of thinking tools as shown in the various Cooperative Learning Teams. These tools were extremely valuable, as they enabled the students to access the curriculum and to transfer their learning from LOTS to HOTS. For this to work, it is critical that the teacher introduces these thinking tools prior to the commencement of this unit. A detailed coverage of these tools is provided in *The Thinking School: Implementing Thinking Skills Across the School* (Pirozzo 2013).
- The groups of four students worked better overall than the groups of only three students.
- As stated above, three gifted students did not work well within their Cooperative Learning Teams. The good news is that while most of the students were completing the work as indicated in the various Cooperative Learning Teams, these three students could have been provided with Ability Grouping, Learning Contracts or Individual Learning Plans.

References

Bossert, ST 1988–1989, 'Cooperative activities in the classroom', *Review of Research in Education,* vol. 15, pp. 225-252.

Cohen, EG 1994, 'Restructuring the classroom: Conditions for productive small groups' *Review of Educational Research*, vol. 64, pp. 1–35.

Gilles, RM & Adrian, F 2003, *Cooperative Learning: The Social and Intellectual Outcomes of Learning in Groups*, Farmers Press, London.

Johnson, D, Johnson RW & Holubec E 1992, *Advanced Cooperative Learning*, rev. edn, Interaction Book Company, Edina, MN.

Johnson, D, Johnson RW & Smith K 1991, *Active Learning: Cooperation in the college classroom*. Edina, MN: Interaction Book Company.

Kagan, S 1994, *Cooperative Learning*, Kagan Publishing, San Clemente, CA.

Macpherson, A 2000–2007, *Cooperative Learning: Group Activities for College Courses*, Kwantlen University College, http://www1.umn.edu/ohr/prod/groups/ohr/@pub/@ohr/documents/asset/ohr_89185.pdf.

Pirozzo, R 2013, *The Thinking School: Implementing Thinking Skills Across the School,* Hawker Brownlow Education, Melbourne, Victoria.

Slavin, RE 1990, *Cooperative Learning; Theory, Research and Practice*, Allyn and Bacon, Toronto, Canada.

Tuckman, BW 1965, 'Developmental sequence in small groups', *Psychological Bulletin*, vol. 63, no. 6, pp. 384–399.

Tuckman, BW & Jensen MC 1997, 'Stages of small-group development revisited', *Group and Organization Studies*, vol. 2, no. 4, pp. 419–427.

Chapter 3
Learning Contracts

A Learning Contract is a written agreement between a student and a teacher. By enabling students to choose the activities they would like to complete, they can produce evidence that these activities have been completed in order to attain a certain level of achievement. Learning Contracts encourage students to take responsibility for their own learning, thus becoming less dependent on teachers. Becoming an active, responsible and self-directed learner is the cornerstone of Learning Contracts.

In my book *17 Learning Contracts* (Pirozzo 2012), I stated that teachers could use Learning Contracts to thrive in classrooms where the range of abilities and learning styles in students can be extremely varied. Thus, Learning Contracts can be used to:

- provide students with the opportunity to choose the activities they would like to do in order to achieve a certain level of achievement
- improve students' commitment to work
- encourage students to develop better working habits by monitoring their own progress
- allow students to take responsibility for their own learning

Other researchers such as Anderson, Boud and Sampson (1996), Knowles (1986), Laycock and Stephenson (1994) and Wilson and Cutting (2001) have reported similar results in relation to the impact of Learning Contracts on students' learning. The question still remains of how teachers who have not had the opportunity to implement this strategy should go about doing it.

For in-depth coverage of the 17 Learning Contracts with all teachers' reflections, the reader is encouraged to read the book titled *17 Learning Contracts*. The teachers that kindly contributed their units to *17 Learning Contracts* were invited to provide their reflections. This is a selection of their stories.

Shannon Wasmann – Years 1–3

Learning Contracts allow children to work at their own pace and ability level, giving them the opportunity to complete tasks that are of interest to them. My students love working on a matrix as a whole-term theme – they are engaged and feel a great deal of accomplishment when they see the amount of work they have completed.

Ross Middleton – Year 4 teaching principal

Depending on the contract design, students can be offered varying lengths of contracts, coupled with formats for presenting the end results. This type of flexibility has a myriad of advantages for classes, as the teacher can better cater to different interests and learning styles through the contract learning design, while still addressing the syllabus outcomes.

Henrietta Miller – Year 5

My class love the freedom that Learning Contracts give them – they feel empowered by the notion of choice and they love choosing what to work on. Student engagement is never a problem and the use of these contracts are always looked forward to and welcomed. Having said that, I've had problems guiding gifted children to choose appropriate tasks. It seems that at Year 5 level, most of them will still gravitate towards easier tasks. At times I have also needed to set limits on the style of tasks chosen to avoid a student always picking the same type of group task, therefore not actually completing anything in depth. I have no real discipline problems in my class, but Learning Contracts are seen as fun, so that helps.

Steve Paslawskyj – Year 5 and 6

The biggest benefit that I have noticed has been with children who are less independent learners. This is mainly because the expectations and requirements are clearly defined for them, so they know explicitly what is required of them and what they have to do to attain a certain level of achievement.

Using Learning Contracts in the classroom requires children to exert greater levels of self-discipline. Initially, I thought this may have been an issue and some children may have slipped through the cracks by not being committed to their learning, but it was quite the opposite. Children who were renowned for falling behind, working slowly and not completing tasks relished the opportunity to work at their own pace and learn things that they were interested in, resulting in an enormous improvement in their achievements.

I have always believed that much of the time spent in the classroom on discipline issues is a result of children not being interested in what they are learning, or being bored because what they are doing is too easy. Learning Contracts provide a solution to both of these issues, as students don't have to complete tasks or learn about things they are not interested in, and they can be challenged through the varying levels of difficulty required for them to perform at the top level.

Scott Crompton – Year 6

I saw a significant improvement in the amount of engagement in work. The students drive the activities and are interested and enthused about the learning and completing tasks. They are excited to move onto the next engagement. The higher order activities take the students further than basic understanding, and they're challenged to develop much higher levels of thinking to complete these activities. Some students need to be led along the path, while others thrive on the freedom to experiment and extend themselves.

Discipline becomes less of an issue if the grid is designed to cater to all students, and there always seems to be something for everyone. The strugglers tend to learn from the high flyers as they do the more challenging tasks and are keen to help out. Perhaps the biggest issue is trying to keep the class quiet, as they tend to be bustling with energy and excitement as they go about their tasks. A lot of this is interacting with each other and sharing what they are doing.

Vicki French – Year 7 English

Students are more engaged because they are involved with the selection of the activities that they choose to do and their depth of learning is greater. By offering a variety of activities based on different learning styles, teachers also offer a challenge to students to learn in different ways. Students who are able to learn through a variety of ways are more effective learners. By creating positive learning experiences, students are more likely to engage in higher-order thinking and by helping them develop their higher order thinking skills, we are helping them to fulfil their potential.

There are far less discipline problems because students have chosen the activities they want to do and are more interested in the task. With the activities suited to different preferred ways of learning, students know they will achieve success and are less likely to be distracted from the task. Students usually only misbehave if they are bored, frustrated, confused or do not know what to do. The contract helps to build a positive relationship through individual help and collaboration and this, in turn, results in engaged, busy learning.

Melissa McGrath – Year 7 English

Lessons are busy and students work together, discussing their findings and experiences. They are so engaged that discipline becomes more about containing enthusiasm rather than battling with non-compliance. There's an enormous amount of content being covered and shared, and I feel privileged to see that students are excited about their own learning, taking pride in sharing it with others. This type of learning allows peers to acknowledge and praise each other, creating a very supportive and cohesive classroom environment.

Teachers using this method gain a better understanding of how students are motivated and how they learn best. The writing generated in my classroom astounds me at times, as students use the tools of learning to tap into their imagination and develop ideas. The learning tools and framework of the matrix has helped to develop the potential of every child in my classroom.

Debbie Locke – Year 7 head of history

I have two classes using the grids at the moment – a Year 7 and a Year 9. The Year 9 is very successful and I feel all the students are actively working towards completing a set number of tasks. I set the ground rules with them at the beginning:

- They had to be actively working on a task.

- Thirty points worth of activities needed to be completed by the end of term.
- They could do more, not less.

The Year 7 class has been a little different. I have a very strong band of precocious, intelligent, jumpy boys who do better with activities as opposed to just sitting, and who rarely listen to instructions. They like choosing activities, but I have to do a fair bit of pushing and coaxing. I am still working on my directions and negotiation in this class.

Charon Joubert – Year 7 science

Working with students to choose their tasks was most rewarding, since it meant spending time with each student or a small group of students. Many students lacked the confidence to choose tasks from the higher end of the grid, but helping them to think outside the square and attempt something different got them on their way, and then there was no stopping them. It gave me much more freedom as a teacher to facilitate rather than to simply teach. The thinking skills included in the grid assisted students to structure and order their thinking to make more sense of the information they were researching.

I learnt that children like to find out things for themselves. When they are given the freedom to work in their own time, at their own pace, they rise to the occasion and surprise themselves as well as their teachers. The Learning Contract gives students structure, but also freedom to learn.

Nicole Crowe – Year 8 head of physical education

Using this method of teaching has decreased the discipline issues in class, predominantly through the implementation of quality teaching strategies. Students are engaged, have a supportive and creative environment and activities to choose from which are significant and relevant to their physical and learning environment. This strategy is also highly student-directed, therefore the teacher is more able to move around among the students to gauge the completion of work, as well as assist students with any issues.

Implementing Learning Contracts

Learning Contracts should be implemented in four steps. These were followed in constructing the Learning Contract titled 'Why Learn About Plants?' for a Year 7 class (see Figure 22).

1. Use the matrix to set up Learning Contract

By using the matrix to set up Learning Contracts, the teacher can easily detect whether or not the students will have any choices (these are the activities coloured in white squares) and whether the students will be working in both the Lower Order Thinking Skills (LOTS) and the Higher Order Thinking Skills (HOTS). The LOTS are represented by the activities listed under Knowing, Understanding and Applying, while the HOTS activities are listed under Analysing, Creating and Evaluating.

Chapter 3 - Learning Contracts

The 48 Grid Planning Matrix
Why Learn About Plants?

Year Level: 7

Multiple Intelligences	Bloom's Taxonomy: Thinking Levels					
	Knowing (1 cp)	**Understanding (2 cp)**	**Applying (3 cp)**	**Analysing (4 cp)**	**Creating (5 cp)**	**Evaluating (6 cp)**
VERBAL — I enjoy reading, writing and speaking	Are plants of any value to us? **Thinking clouds**	Is chlorophyll similar or different to other pigments? Explain!	Prepare a report on your experiment on photosynthesis experiment. **GLOW**	Construct a poster to show the various stages of photosynthesis. **TAP**	Create a radio or TV ad to promote the importance of photosynthesis. **BROW**	Review the book titled _____ and recommend how to grow the best crops in _____.
MATHEMATICAL — I enjoy working with numbers and science	What is photosynthesis? YouTube: *My fave song: The photosynthesis song*.	Write the word formula for photosynthesis.	Carry out an experiment to see if plants need light for photosynthesis. **PSDR**	Analyse your experiment and then carry out a **LDC** on it.	Predict which factors would increase the rate of photosynthesis.	Research and justify your prediction in relation to photosynthesis.
VISUAL/SPATIAL — I enjoy painting, drawing and visualising	Look at a number of different plants. Are they the same?	Explain the size of leaves from plants that thrive in the: • tropics • deserts	Draw and label a cross section of a leaf using a microscope.	Compare and contrast photosynthesis during day and in the night.	Design and build a model of a stomata. **TAP**	Use this model to teach another student. Did it work? How do you know? Can you improve it? **SCRAM**
KINAESTHETIC — I enjoy doing hands-on activities, sports and dance	Participate in a field trip to the local environmental education centre.	Name the various organisms that live on leaves.	Collect and sort various organisms that live on leaves.	Prepare a **Venn diagram** of a cactus plant and an umbrella tree.	Construct a model of photosynthesis that can be used to teach others.	Devise a board game titled 'photosynthesis' and prepare a manual.
MUSICAL — I enjoy making and listening to music	Select and listen to a number of songs that relate to forests.	Do plants grow better in areas where music is played? Explain.	Present data relating to the impact that music may have on plant growth.	Write two raps, jingles or songs about plants and their growth.	Add the relevant music to your raps, jingles or songs.	Use **LDC** to evaluate how appropriate this music is for your audience.
INTERPERSONAL — I enjoy working with others	What are plant pigments used for? **TAP**	Research at least five different types of plant pigments.	With another student, design an experiment on photosynthesis.	Working in groups, examine leaf size to adaptation.	Working with two other students, construct a terrarium.	Interview a farmer about the various herbicides used in her/his farm.
INTRAPERSONAL — I enjoy working by myself	What will happen to plants if the sun stops shining?	If spring does not arrive, how will plants cope? **Y Chart**	How will trees feel when they are chopped down? **X Chart**	Analyse data on the impact of deforestation on the water cycle.	Predict what will happen to plant growth if CO^2 increases greatly?	Use **SOWC** to forecast the impact of logging on the water cycle.
NATURALIST — I enjoy caring for plants and animals	What would your life be without plants and animals?	Explain why some animals, such as the koala, survive only on the leaves of certain eucalyptus trees.	Make a collection of plants and/or animals that are available in your local area.	Organise a marketing campaign to prevent logging in the major rainforests of the world.	Create one of the following: • recycling program • mulching station • vegetable garden	Evaluate your project using **LDC**. Now, list any changes that can be made to improve your project.

Content descriptions/learning outcomes/the essential learnings:

Figure 22

2. Devise an appropriate point system and relevant assessment guidelines

Devise a point system by adding your selected credit points underneath Bloom's Taxonomy: Thinking Levels. This is how I prefer to allocate credit points: Knowing (1), Understanding (2), Applying (3), Analysing (4), Creating (5) Evaluating (6). This can be seen in the matrix in Figure 22. Not all teachers will use the same credit point system, so just find something that can be clearly understood and indicates that the more difficult activities are valued higher than the less difficult ones.

The teacher should devote some time in explaining that regardless of which multiple intelligence they work within, all the activities listed under, for example, Knowing are valued 1 credit point. The same will apply to the remaining levels of thinking.

It's time to take the students through the actual Learning Contract. Teachers should ensure parents or guardians are aware of the use of Learning Contracts. A Learning Contract should be signed by the student, parent/guardian and the teacher. Ensure that this is done prior to commencement, as some parents may object to signing such a document.

As stated in the figure below, the points needed for students to be awarded a certain level of achievement needs to align with your school's assessment guidelines. In primary schools, you'll check with your principal, assistant principal or head of curriculum. We've found that in secondary schools, the head of department or head of curriculum is usually the best person to confer with regarding these matters.

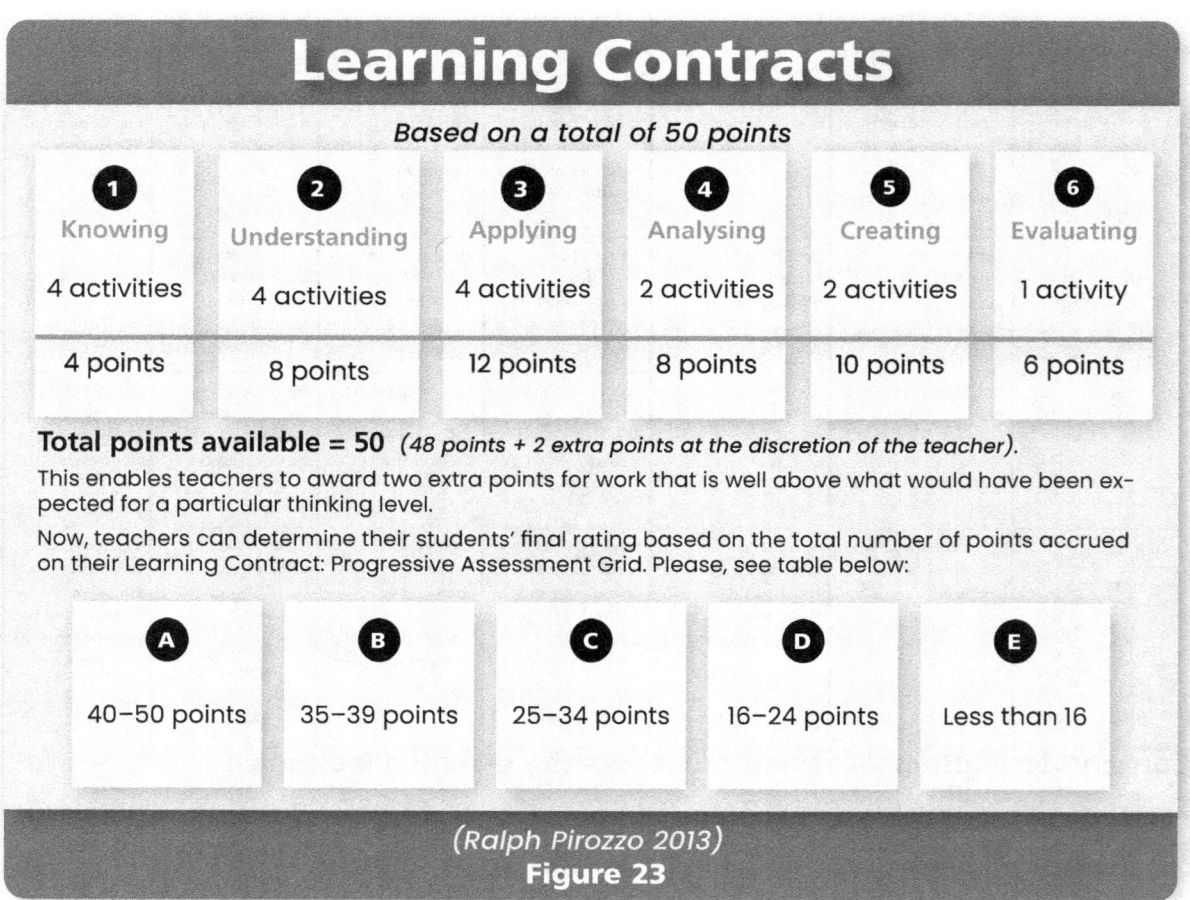

(Ralph Pirozzo 2013)
Figure 23

Learning Contract

Why Learn About Plants?

DUE DATE / /

- This Learning Contract will provide you with plenty of choices, however, you will need to use your time very wisely!

- The blue squares are core activities and will be completed by your teacher with the whole class through explicit teaching. Note that these do not count towards your credit points. It is critical that you constantly conference with your teacher.

- No more than 50 per cent of your points should come from your RAMP (your three preferred multiple intelligences).

- You will be given class and library time as well as being able to work on certain tasks at home.

- You must have your contract with you at school every day.

- You are to choose your tasks from at least three thinking levels and at least three different intelligences

- Activities shaded in yellow will attract additional bonus points.

- In order to be awarded your chosen level of achievement you must achieve the minimum credit points listed under 'Level of Achievement'. For example, to achieve an A you will have to accumulate a minimum of 40 credit points. Rubrics will be used for assessment purposes.

Knowing: 1 credit point
Understanding: 2 credit points
Applying: 3 credit points

Analysing: 4 credit points
Creating: 5 credit points
Evaluating: 6 credit points

Level of Achievement	A	B	C	D	E
Points needed to be awarded these levels	40–50	35–39	25–34	16–24	Less than 16
Total points achieved					
Final level of achievement					

....
Student Signature   **Parent / Guardian Signature**   **Teacher Signature**

DATE COMPLETED / /

(Ralph Pirozzo 2008)
Figure 24

At this stage, the teacher needs to talk to each student to make sure that they fully understand the point system, the rubric and that their selection is balanced. This means ensuring that they have selected activities in both the LOTS and HOTS, and in various learning styles. Students need to be reminded that they should select a maximum of 50 per cent of their points from their RAMP (representing their three preferred learning styles).

3. Use rubrics for assessment and reporting purposes

When working on the unit titled 'Why Learn about Plants?', I was working with a Year 7 student named Zac, who quickly chose the activity which allowed him to review the book and recommend how to grow the best crops (Verbal/Evaluating), because this activity would give him six credit points. Zac proceeded to read and review this book in a hurry as if this were a competition of finishing first, regardless of the quality produced. Having spent very little time in analysing the content of the book and not providing an in-depth recommendation on how to grow the best crops in a particular type of soil, Zac approached the teacher with no more than a few notes written on a piece of paper, expecting to receive six credit points. The teacher had to inform Zac that he would not receive six credit points unless he was prepared to significantly improve the quality of his work. At this point, Zac erupted and accused the teacher of not liking him and that he would let his mum know he was being treated unfairly. As expected, Zac's mum did contact the principal the following day and we can predict what happened from there.

All this confrontation and aggravation could have easily been avoided if the teacher had developed a rubric for assessment and reporting purposes, and had shown it to the students prior to working on this Learning Contract. A sample of such a generic rubric can be found on the following page (Figure 25).

Since working with Zac I have never implemented Learning Contracts without first generating a rubric. The rubric should be:

- given to the students as an integral part of their Learning Contract
- posted on the school's website, enabling students, parents and guardians to download it
- placed on the classroom's wall for the duration of the Learning Contract
- used to provide feedback and for assessment and reporting purposes.

Learning Contract – Rubric

STUDENT NAME:

Criteria	Scale of Assessment					Teacher comments
	A	B	C	D	E	
Organisation	Extremely well organised and the main ideas and topics are extremely easy to follow.	Very well organised and the main ideas and topics are very easy to follow.	The organisation of this report is good and the main ideas and topics are easy to follow.	The report is poorly organised and the main ideas and topics are difficult to follow.	The report is very poorly organised and the main ideas and topics are extremely hard to follow.	
Imagination/ Creativity/ Originality	The material is presented in an extremely imaginative, creative and original manner.	The material is presented in a very imaginative, creative and original manner.	The material is presented in a somewhat imaginative, creative and original manner.	The material presented requires more imagination, creativity and originality.	The material presented lacks imagination, creativity and originality.	
Comprehension	Excellent comprehension of the main topic.	Very good comprehension of the main topic.	Good comprehension of the main topic.	Poor comprehension of the main topic.	Very poor comprehension of the main topic.	
Spelling and grammar	The report is free of spelling, grammar and punctuation errors.	The report has few spelling, grammar and punctuation errors.	The report has a number of spelling, grammar and punctuation errors.	The report is full of spelling, grammar and punctuation errors.	The report is poorly written and difficult to read.	
Presentation	The report is extremely well presented.	The report is well presented.	The presentation is good.	The presentation is poor.	It is presented in an extremely poor manner.	

Demonstrated Scale of Assessment: _____ **Date:** _____ **Teacher:** _____

(Ralph Pirozzo, 2012)
Figure 25

4. Track students' progress

Imagine that now we have 30 Year 7 students busily working on their Learning Contracts! Each student has selected their own activities in order to attain a particular achievement level and somehow the teacher has to keep all this information in their heads. Unnecessarily placing teachers under pressure is the last thing we want, so to make tracking students' progress easy to achieve, we have developed the 'Learning Contract: Progressive Assessment Grid'.

Learning Contract: Progressive Assessment Grid

NAME OF UNIT: _____ YEAR LEVEL: _____ STUDENT NAME: _____

Date	Learning Activity	Points Gained					Comments	Scales of Assessment				
		1	2	3	4	5 and 6		A	B	C	D	E
								Gather all the assessment tasks completed by this student. Then use your professional judgement, based on the relevant rubrics, to determine this student's final Level of Achievement.				

Overall comments: _____

Learning activities completed: _____

Teacher's signature: _____

Total points: _____ Date: _____ Final level of achievement: _____

(Devised by Ralph Pirozzo in 1997 and updated in 2012)
Figure 26

For this assessment grid to work effectively, teachers should do the following:

- Make two copies – one for the students to keep and one for their own records.

- As students complete activities, they will discuss with their teachers who, based on the rubric, will determine the number of credit points to be awarded. For example, Zac chose an activity valued at six credit points, however, based on the rubric and the quality of work produced, he would only receive two credit points. This ensures that Zac understands that to be given six credit points, his work would have to meet the criteria stated in the rubric. In the 'points gained' column, Zac would score two instead of a six. It's important to address that, just because a student has chosen an activity of six credit points, they will not receive full points unless their work meets the criteria in the rubric. This can be a rather difficult concept for students and parents to grasp, who may equate quantity over quality to the awarding of points. It's important that students understand that, just because they've chosen an activity valued at six credit points, they will not receive full marks unless the work is in line with the rubric.

    With a challenging student like Zac, the teacher should go to the 'comments' column and write the time and the date when this discussion took place, and that Zac was advised he would only receive two credit points for his work. Zac should also be given the opportunity to resubmit his work to improve his marks, which should also be recorded, as well as the fact that the teacher would be willing to assist him in doing so. Zac now has two choices – leave his work as is and receive two credit points out of a maximum of six, or improve his work with the help of his teacher and re-submit in the hope of receiving a higher score.

    By the time the teacher has completed 'comments' column, they will have a huge amount of objective data (including the time and the date that they have conferenced with their students). This will serve them well in the event that a student and/or parent were to challenge their professional judgment and integrity. This is accountability at its very best and its value should not be underestimated.

- At the end of the Learning Contract, teachers should add up all credit points and determine the students' final levels of achievement based on the school's own standards. For example, at this school a student would only be awarded an A if they had accumulated a minimum of 40 credit points.

- Finally, the teacher should complete the remaining items in 'Learning Contract: Progressive Assessment Grid' (Figure 26). Under the overall comments, teachers have the opportunity to improve their students' self-esteem. For example, why wouldn't a teacher let parents know that their son/daughter had worked extremely well and helped the teacher throughout the Learning Contract? In this same class we had a student named Mary, who, even with her learning difficulties, was a most diligent worker and couldn't do enough to help her teacher and the other students.

- Parents like to know the learning activities that their children have completed, the total points accrued and the final level of achievement awarded.

Reflection

Similar to other workers, I've found that the quality of students' work improved significantly by using Learning Contracts. Here are some of my reflections after implementing them in classrooms:

- I saw significant improvements in overall academic performance, working independently, depth and breadth of learning, self-esteem and confidence, intrinsic motivation, critical and creative thinking and problem-solving skills. In particular, this Learning Contract maximised the learning potential of gifted and talented students, very competitive learners and boys.

  It is believed that these gains occur because Learning Contracts provide students with structure, while simultaneously giving them the freedom to choose activities that they are interested in. I never fail to be amazed by the quality of work produced by some students who are not given credit for being able to perform highly in the traditional classroom. Also, many students would continue to complete additional activities even though they have already received an A as their final achievement level. Talk about intrinsic motivation!

- Discipline was not a problem, as the students were totally engaged in completing their chosen activities. As pointed out by Year 7 English teacher, Melissa McGrath, discipline becomes more about containing enthusiasm rather than battling with non-compliance.

- The students found the Learning and Teaching Wheel and The Engaging Wheel particularly useful in discovering their preferred learning styles and why the points allotted to each activity differed (due to the amount of effort required).

- The teacher taught the explicit teaching activities to all students, as it was considered critical information. The rest of the time was spent monitoring students as they completed activities from their Learning Contracts, assessing the activities using the relevant rubric and completing the students' individual Progressive Assessment Grids. It is very important that the teacher conferences with each student at least twice during every session involving Learning Contracts. At any given moment the teacher needs to know exactly what students are doing, and how well they are progressing.

- The students had access to a large number of thinking tools, which were extremely valuable, as they enabled the students to access the curriculum and to transfer their learning from LOTS to HOTS. For this to work, it is critical that the teacher introduces these thinking tools prior to the commencement of this unit. As mentioned earlier, detailed coverage of these thinking tools is provided in *The Thinking School: Implementing Thinking Skills Across the School* (Pirozzo 2013).

- For students considered to be perfectionists, it is advisable to give them a rough estimate in relation to the amount of time they should be devoting to each activity. This will prevent these students from spending so much time in completing some of the activities in the LOTS, thus inadvertently running out of time and not being able to complete many in the HOTS. This can easily be done on the matrix by adding the number of minutes, in brackets, next to each activity.

- There is no effective learning and teaching strategy that is going to be perfect for all students and teachers, and Learning Contracts are no exception. For example, there are teachers who are not willing to provide Learning Contracts to their students based on the fear that they may lose control of the class, and because this methodology doesn't suit their teaching style. In addition, there are parents who refuse to sign their children's Learning Contracts and demand that their children complete their work through what they describe as 'real teaching'. By this they mean having students take notes written by the teacher who stands at the front of the room. This is still considered an integral part of the teaching repertoire – some notes need to be taken while the teacher covers the explicit teaching activities (coloured blue or dark grey in the matrix). In this unit there are no designated Real Assessment Tasks (RATs), as the students will receive the relevant achievement levels by completing their chosen activities. This is an exception to the rule, as every unit should have a certain number of RATs.

We don't believe that Learning Contracts are likely to be an appropriate strategy for students with learning difficulties, EAL/D learners and disadvantaged students unless the teacher can rely on some in-class support. Teacher assistants, enrichment teachers, parents and other teaching and non-teaching personnel can provide this support. If this support is not available, the teacher will be stretched to effectively and efficiently monitor the students' progress and provide individual assistance to these students. Thus, we believe that these types of students' learning needs can be better met by implementing Cooperative Learning Teams, Multi-age Grouping and Individual Learning Plans.

I am grateful to Shannon Wasmann, Ross Middleton, Henrietta Miller, Steve Paslawskyj, Scott Compton, Vicki French, Melissa McGrath, Debbie Locke, Charon Joubert and Nicole Crowe for giving me their permission to include their units in the book titled *17 Learning Contracts*.

References

Anderson, G, Boud D & Sampson J 1996, *Learning Contracts: A Practical Guide*, Kogan Page, London.

Knowles, MS 1986, *Using Learning Contracts*. Jossey-Bass, San Francisco, CA.

Laycock, M & Stephenson J 1994, *Using Learning Contracts in Higher Education*, Kogan Page, London.

Pirozzo, R 2012, *17 Learning Contracts*, Promoting Learning International, Brisbane, Australia.

Wilson, J & Cutting L 2001, *Contracts for Independent Learning*, Education Services Australia, Melbourne, Victoria.

Chapter 4
Learning Centres

A Learning Centre refers to a designated area in the classroom or an organised station on a desktop where students working individually or in small groups complete a specified number of tasks within a precise time frame. The underlying philosophy of Learning Centres is that they encourage students to 'learn by doing'. This enables students to actively construct knowledge by interacting with different materials and with other students.

Barrett (1996) refers to Learning Centres as specific areas in the classroom where students explore a range of ideas and materials together and arrive at the solution to a problem independently. Through such challenges, students are able to exercise choice, take responsibility for their decision-making and work at their own pace.

Others refer to Learning Centres as distinct interest areas in a classroom that offer various materials and opportunities for hands-on learning at individually appropriate levels (Copple & Bredekamp 2006; Epstein 2007).

Baker (2013) says that Learning Centres facilitate both collaboration and independent learning by enabling students to work independently of the teacher. In relation to Musical Learning Centres, Baker argues that they should be seen as discrete physical spaces in the classroom where students may compose, create, perform or listen.

Stuber (2007) reports that since teachers must devote much of their time addressing specific curriculum content, they feel that they have less time to establish and maintain Learning Centres. Many believe that these centres use valuable time and prevent them from covering specific content as required by the mandated standards. However, Stuber argues that when shown that centres are effective teaching and learning approaches, teachers will intentionally develop and integrate hands-on exploratory child and adult-guided learning experiences.

Teachers have been using Learning Centres for a long time. In fact, I was introduced to them while completing my university studies in Canada. At that time they were called Learning Stations. However, the growth and acceptance of Learning Centres increased greatly after the publication of Howard Gardner's book titled *Frames of Mind* in 1983. Undeniably, Gardener's Multiple Intelligence Theory provides a very strong theoretical base on which to structure Learning Centres.

Multiple Intelligence Theory further supports the notion that each individual is unique. Once we recognise that each student has their own set of intellectual strengths and weaknesses, teachers are in a position to structure the way they present new material to engage all their students. Indeed, one of the most remarkable features of Multiple Intelligence Theory is how it provides teachers with eight possible pathways to engage students.

Implementing Learning Centres

Traditionally, teachers implement Learning Centres to:

- engage students in learning
- better meet the needs of individual students by taking into consideration their knowledge, skills and interests
- utilise a variety of strategies to provide for each student's preferred learning styles
- allow students to learn through self-discovery and take responsibility for their learning
- promote independence in students, allowing them to become more responsible
- increase motivation in students
- allow students to inquire, investigate, explore and record their learning
- give students the opportunity for hands-on practice while developing social skills by working in small groups
- work with students in small groups or one-on-one to target specific skills. For example, a teacher may have a student spending more time in the Mathematical Learning Centre to build skills in a specific area of mathematics
- integrate multiple subjects so learning happens in a meaningful context
- assess students' understanding and knowledge through observation and authentic assessment
- create a student-centred (rather than teacher-centred) learning environment
- review basic skills
- foster a love of learning and become a facilitator of learning

Prior to setting up their Learning Centres, teachers should identify the skills they want their students to develop. Once this has been accomplished, they should determine:

- the number of Learning Centres to be created
- the materials needed in each Learning Centre, and how to familiarise the students with the materials they will be using in each Learning Centre
- how to display the material, e.g. on top of tables, placed in folders, on a USB or an organised station on a desktop
- a list of rules and behaviour to be taught before work in the Learning Centres commences, to be posted in a place where the students can see them
- if students are to work individually or in small groups. The groups should be kept to three or four students, enabling students to complete tasks on time and to be able to easily move to the next station
- clear directions and signage so students know which centre to go to next
- an established rotation pattern with a time limit so students move freely from one centre to another, giving everyone a turn
- a particular phrase, hand-clap or bell to let students know that the time has

come for them to move to the next Learning Centre. It is critical that transition from one station to another occurs on time and in a smooth fashion
- a time to place the relevant materials back to their original position for the next group to use, once the Learning Centre is completed
- a designated area, e.g. a table or a folder for each student, where students place their completed work for marking and assessment

Based on Multiple Intelligence Theory, teachers could have up to eight different Learning Centres operating in their classrooms. However, it's suggested that teachers begin implementing their Learning Centres slowly. It's better at first to have a few Learning Centres operating well than having many that are noisy, chaotic and unproductive.

The way teachers set up their Learning Centres depends greatly on the year level, subject area, amount of space available, number of computers available and the students' own individual learning styles. A list of the kind of materials that students may find in the 'ideal' Learning Centre can be found below.

Verbal Learning Centre

Verbal Learning Centres cater to students' Verbal-Linguistic, Visual-Spatial, Intrapersonal and Interpersonal intelligences. Materials may include:

- children's books with accompanying tapes
- magazine, newspapers, brochures, phone directory
- fiction and non-fiction books on a variety of topics
- various writing utensils such as pens, pencils, crayons, felt-tip pens, coloured pencils
- different types of writing paper, blank booklets, pads
- word cards
- puzzles for constructing words
- magnetic boards
- magnetic or wooden letters and phonograms
- letter cubes and phonograms
- word wall for high-frequency words
- word wheels for constructing words
- word sorting and word building activities
- skill-development games, e.g. Concentration, Jeopardy
- letter stamps
- felt boards and story characters
- cardboard alphabet shapes
- puppets and a small stage
- places for students to display their work
- rugs, throw pillows, bean bags, chairs
- computer with colour printer and access to the Internet

Mathematical Learning Centre

Mathematical Learning Centres cater to students' Logical-Mathematical, Bodily-Kinaesthetic, Intrapersonal-Intuitive and Interpersonal-Social intelligences. Materials may include:

- abacuses and tangrams
- number blocks and laminated numbers for tracing
- calculators
- clocks
- graph paper
- stopwatches, clock stamps and ink pads
- magnetic boards and magnetic numbers
- number stamps and ink pads
- buttons, beads, counters, dice, bingo spinners, counting chips
- puzzles and games that involve logical thinking
- arithmetic and graphing calculators
- maths manipulatives such as Unifix cubes, pattern blocks, Cuisinaire rods
- play money and cash registers
- materials for measuring (tape measure, ruler, yard stick, string)
- assortment of objects for counting (buttons, bottle caps)
- height charts
- scales and different weights
- maps, charts and timelines
- timers
- fraction rubber stamps and pie circles
- computer with colour printer and access to spreadsheets, graphing and two and three-dimensional geometry programs

Science Learning Centre

Science Learning Centres cater to students' Logical-Mathematical, Visual-Spatial, Bodily-Kinaesthetic, Naturalist, Intrapersonal-Intuitive and Interpersonal-Social intelligences. Materials may include:

- science resources
- popular science magazines
- biographies of scientists and inventors
- magnifying glasses, microscopes, telescopes and binoculars
- measuring devices such as rulers, test tubes, graduated cylinders, measuring cups, funnels
- jars, boxes and plastic containers for collecting specimens
- seasonal materials such as leaves, seeds, seashells, insects, snails, pinecones, rocks
- barometers and thermometers

- magnets
- weather charts
- field guides
- life cycle charts
- animal models
- compasses
- spare batteries and light bulbs
- home chemicals (salt, baking soda, vinegar, sugar)
- rain gauges
- computer with colour printer, access to spreadsheets and science-based software and the Internet

Visual/Spatial Learning Centre

Visual Learning Centres cater to students' Visual-Spatial, Bodily-Kinaesthetic, Logical-Mathematical, Intrapersonal-Intuitive and Interpersonal-Social intelligences. Materials may include:

- books on art
- painting materials such as acrylics, watercolours, paints
- drawing materials such as pens, pencils, coloured chalk
- easel, bulletin board, chalk board, drawing boards or tables
- canvases
- washable paints and paint brushes
- water colours
- aprons for cover-up
- coloured water for colour mixing
- glue, scissors, markers, coloured pencils
- clay and play dough
- washable ink pads and stamps
- several types of paper, including large paper for murals
- items for collages
- props and cameras
- computer with colour printer, scanner and Internet connection

Kinaesthetic Learning Centre

Kinaesthetic Learning Centres cater to students' Bodily-Kinaesthetic, Visual-Spatial, Logical-Mathematical, Intrapersonal-Intuitive and Interpersonal-Social intelligences. Materials may include:

- glue, scissors, staplers, nails, screws, pins, clips
- recycled materials such as wood, metals, containers, bottles
- coloured paper and cardboard boxes

- markers and crayons
- fabric scraps
- modelling clay
- wigs, costumes, masks and washable makeup
- puppets and a small stage
- a cooking station, which could have:
  - a variety of cooking books
  - cutlery, utensils, crockery and materials such as baking tray, measuring cups, mixers
  - flour, sugar, salt, rice, potatoes, herbs
  - access to microwave ovens and cleaning facilities
- a sewing station, which could have:
  - a variety of books on sewing and sewing patterns
  - measuring tapes, templates, rulers
  - sewing kits, scissors, needles, threads, fabrics
  - access to sewing machines
- computer with colour printer, scanner, Internet connection and design software such as CAD-CAM (Computer Assisted Design-Computer Assisted Manufacturing) software for older students

Musical Learning Centre

Musical Learning Centres cater to students' Musical-Rhythmic, Bodily-Kinaesthetic, Logical-Mathematical, Intrapersonal-Intuitive and Interpersonal-Social intelligences. Materials may include:

- books about famous composers and musicians
- a selection of music
- speakers and earphones for individual listening centres
- musical instruments
- materials that students can use to make musical instruments such as tipping sticks, hand bells, shakers, chopsticks, beads, string, spoons, tape, plastic bottles, rubber bands, uncooked rice, empty shoe boxes, paper towel rolls, unwaxed paper
- poems and stories that students can set music to
- computers with Internet access, microphones, musical composition software, CD-ROMs for music study and software to incorporate sound into multimedia presentations

Naturalist Learning Centre

Naturalist Learning Centres cater to students' Naturalist, Logical-Mathematical, Visual-Spatial, Bodily-Kinaesthetic, Intrapersonal-Intuitive and Interpersonal-Social intelligences. Materials may include:

- field guides and science resources
- barometers and thermometers
- magnifying glasses, microscopes, telescopes and binoculars
- measurement devices such as rulers, test tubes, graduated cylinders, funnels, measuring cups
- jars, boxes, plastic containers for collecting specimens
- natural specimens such as insects, flowers and rocks for classification
- seasonal materials such as leaves, seeds, seashells, insects, snails, pine cones, rocks
- gardening tools such as small hoes, buckets, shovels, rakes, watering cans
- a variety of vegetable seeds
- a variety of plants
- small animals such as chickens or guinea pigs to raise and care for
- aquarium and terrarium
- sections of tree trunks
- animal models
- life cycle charts
- weather charts
- rain gauges and weather stations
- planting projects in association with your local branch of Greening Australia (see *www.greeningaustralia.org.au*)
- recycling projects such as mulching, composting and establishing a small organic garden
- individual nature portfolios to store students' animal and plant specimens, field notes, drawing and photos
- computer with colour printer, access to spreadsheets and nature-based software and Internet

You may have noticed that we have not listed any intrapersonal or interpersonal Learning Centres. It's felt that students will develop their intrapersonal and/or interpersonal intelligences given the fact that they have the opportunity to complete the work in all Learning Centres either individually or in groups.

However, in case of very shy and introverted students, the teacher may have to set up a station in a secluded part of the classroom where these students could work by themselves without being interrupted by the other students. It is hoped that as these students get used to have Learning Centres operating in their classroom, that slowly they will join other students.

We have dealt with the theory that underpins the reasons why they exist and what students are likely to find in an idealised or theoretical Learning Centre. However, teachers do not live in an idealised or theoretical world, and in a real classroom they need to cater to students displaying a very wide range of abilities, interests and learning styles, while acknowledging the fact that they also have their own preferred teaching styles.

Implementing Learning Centres

To see how this can be done, two very different units and their corresponding Learning Centres will be profiled:

1. 'The Very Hungry Caterpillar' (Foundation) – created by Pip Riordan and Ros Mangold
2. 'Marketing Your Boat' (Year 9 Science Class)

Both units are based on the matrix so that at a glance, the teacher can see whether or not they promote Lower Order Thinking Skills (LOTS) and Higher Thinking Skills (HOTS), and if the students are likely to have any choices (white squares).

Some activities have been coloured in yellow (light grey in book). As usual, these are the Real Assessment Tasks (RATs) that the students need to complete. The teacher will collect the RATs for marking, assessment and reporting purposes.

In both instances we see a number next to each activity. This represents the scope and sequence – the order that the activities could be completed. For example, Activity 2 should be attempted after the students have completed Activity 1 and so on. For the Year 9 activities, the numbers are to be considered to be a guide, as the students can alter the way they will complete the relevant RAT.

These two units differ in terms of the amount of explicit teaching to be done (blue or dark grey activities). By looking at the Foundation (prep) unit 'The Very Hungry Caterpillar', one realises that there is a significant amount of explicit teaching required. Given the young age of these students, this is exactly what one would expect. The Year 9 students did not require a great deal of explicit teaching, however, I did have to regularly review the thinking tools that the students were expected to use in completing this unit. This was done prior to the students commencing work in the Learning Centres.

In relation to both units, we know the activities students will be completing, the RATS, the activities in both LOTS and HOTS, the explicit teaching and the order that the activities should be completed. What we do not know, as yet is how the Foundation students reacted to this unit and the respective Learning Centres.

The Very Hungry Caterpillar – Foundation (prep)

The teachers who created this unit, Pip Riordan and Ros Mangold explain in an email from 1 January, 2014 how they found themselves team-teaching the unit based on the popular children's book *The Very Hungry Caterpillar* to 40 Foundation students in the school library.

> While Eric Carle's *The Very Hungry Caterpillar* had always been a popular teaching tool, we wanted to use it as a focus to integrate a history/social unit on personal needs and a science unit on animal needs and life cycles. The aim was to create a learning environment that promoted independent learning, while using differentiated activities to cater to a wide variety of student needs.
>
> The spacious library allowed us to spread the Learning Centres around the room for students to access independently during the morning literacy sessions. While we focused on the modelled and guided aspects of teaching reading and writing, the students independently completed both compulsory activities that were designated based on their learning needs, and free choice activities to consolidate prior learning.
>
> The most popular activity had the children reassemble a butterfly as a jigsaw. To ensure the activity's success, we:
>
> - laminated multiple copies and cut up into pieces of body parts, i.e. head, wings, legs
> - used matching and labelling activities where the students place the labels on the correct body parts. Sometimes they photocopy the butterfly and use it as an assessment task for body part labels
> - used the butterfly picture as a talking or writing stimulus for students to describe the butterfly either in words or writing
> - compared the picture to a moth and discussed differences and similarities between them
>
> We found that the students were highly motivated and eager to achieve their personal best during this unit. They also demonstrated improved independence and interpersonal skills across all key learning areas and throughout the whole school day. Their deep knowledge of the content was still apparent later in the year, well beyond the completion of the unit.
>
> As a result of the success of this unit, our school will continue to use it on a yearly basis, with regular tweaks and variations to suit new cohorts. We believe this way of teaching and learning gives each student the opportunity to achieve their own best within an engaging and active learning environment.

The Learning Centres used in this unit can be found on the following pages.

The 56 Grid Planning Matrix - The Very Hungry Caterpillar

By Pip Riordan Ros Mangold Year Level: Foundation

Bloom's Taxonomy: Thinking Levels

Multiple Intelligences	Pre-Knowing	Knowing	Understanding	Applying	Analysing	Creating	Evaluating
VERBAL I enjoy reading, writing and speaking	2. Brainstorm what they know about caterpillars. Thinking clouds	1. Read *The Very Hungry Caterpillar*. 3. Read a variety of fiction and non-fiction books.	9. Shared reading of a book about caterpillars.	Illustrate a word from the vocabulary list.	**Real Assessment Task 1** Arrange and organise the sequence of events in the life cycle of a butterfly.	As a class, construct an acrostic poem using the word 'butterfly'. - **See Learning Centre 2** Create a menu for an insect that is coming to dinner.	Discuss whether or not insects are good. Review the video of the story and justify.
MATHEMATICAL I enjoy working with numbers and science	Vocabulary: egg, caterpillar, butterfly	Match numeral cards with arrays.		12. How many legs are on an insect?	Sequence the days of the week.	**Real Assessment Task 2** Estimate the total number of legs of a given number of butterflies.	
VISUAL/SPATIAL I enjoy painting, drawing and visualising	cocoon, chrysalis, metamorphosis, pupa, leaf, nectar, pollen, head	11. Label the body parts of the butterfly - **See Learning Centre 1** Draw and label body parts of people.		8. Arrange the life stages of a caterpillar in order.	**Real Assessment Task 3** Create a Venn diagram to compare the needs of a caterpillar/butterfly to those of themselves. - **See Learning Centre 5**	Imagine you are a caterpillar – design a cocoon for yourself. Design your own butterfly wings.	
KINAESTHETIC I enjoy doing hands-on activities, sports and dance	abdomen, thorax, leg, moth, skin	Locate pictures of insects.	Identify syllables in the vocabulary.		Put the pictures in the same order as they appear in the story. - **See Learning Centre 3**	Design and build a three-dimensional insect that has never been seen before.	
MUSICAL I enjoy making and listening to music	water, air, food, shelter, need, emerge	Listen to music.	Learn a new song: 'Caterpillar, Caterpillar'.	Make a song or jingle about caterpillars in a group.	What part of your song or jingle do you like the most? Sing it to the entire class and receive their feedback.	Based on your class' feedback, work with your group to create your final song or jingle about caterpillars.	Who would be interested in hearing you sing your song or jingle about caterpillars? Discuss.
INTERPERSONAL I enjoy working with others	hatch, crawl, eat, lay, spin	Locate and copy vocabulary with magnetic letters.	5. With a partner, describe and draw what was seen on the walk.			With a friend, discuss and arrange the events of the story in order.	
INTRAPERSONAL I enjoy working by myself	shed, fly, dry, drink, antennae, wings	Personal writing using the vocabulary list.	What am I? Egg, or caterpillar or butterfly. Read clues and have student hold up the correct card. - **See Learning Centre 4**	6. Write a sentence about your drawing.	Conference with your teacher and receive their comments.	Use the teacher's comments to improve your writing.	Work with your teacher to apply the **LDC** to your writing.
NATURALIST I enjoy caring for plants and animals	4. Walk around the school grounds to find insects.	7. Draw a picture of a caterpillar and its habitat.	10a. Restate needs of insects. Identify personal needs.		10b. Introduce a Venn diagram to compare insect and personal needs.		Whole class discussion on determining and justifying the most important needs of plants.

Figure 27

Learning Centre 1

Figure 28

Level of Thinking: Knowing
Way of Learning: Visual-Spatial, Bodily-Kinaesthetic

Label the body parts of the butterfly.

head   thorax   abdomen   antennae   wings

Learning Centre 2

Figure 29

Level of Thinking: Creating
Way of Learning: Verbal-Linguistic

Create an acrostic poem.

B
U
T
T
E
R
F
L
Y

Chapter 4 - Learning Centres 73

Learning Centre 3

Figure 30

Level of Thinking: Analysing
Way of Learning: Bodily-Kinaesthetic

Put the pictures in the same order as the story.

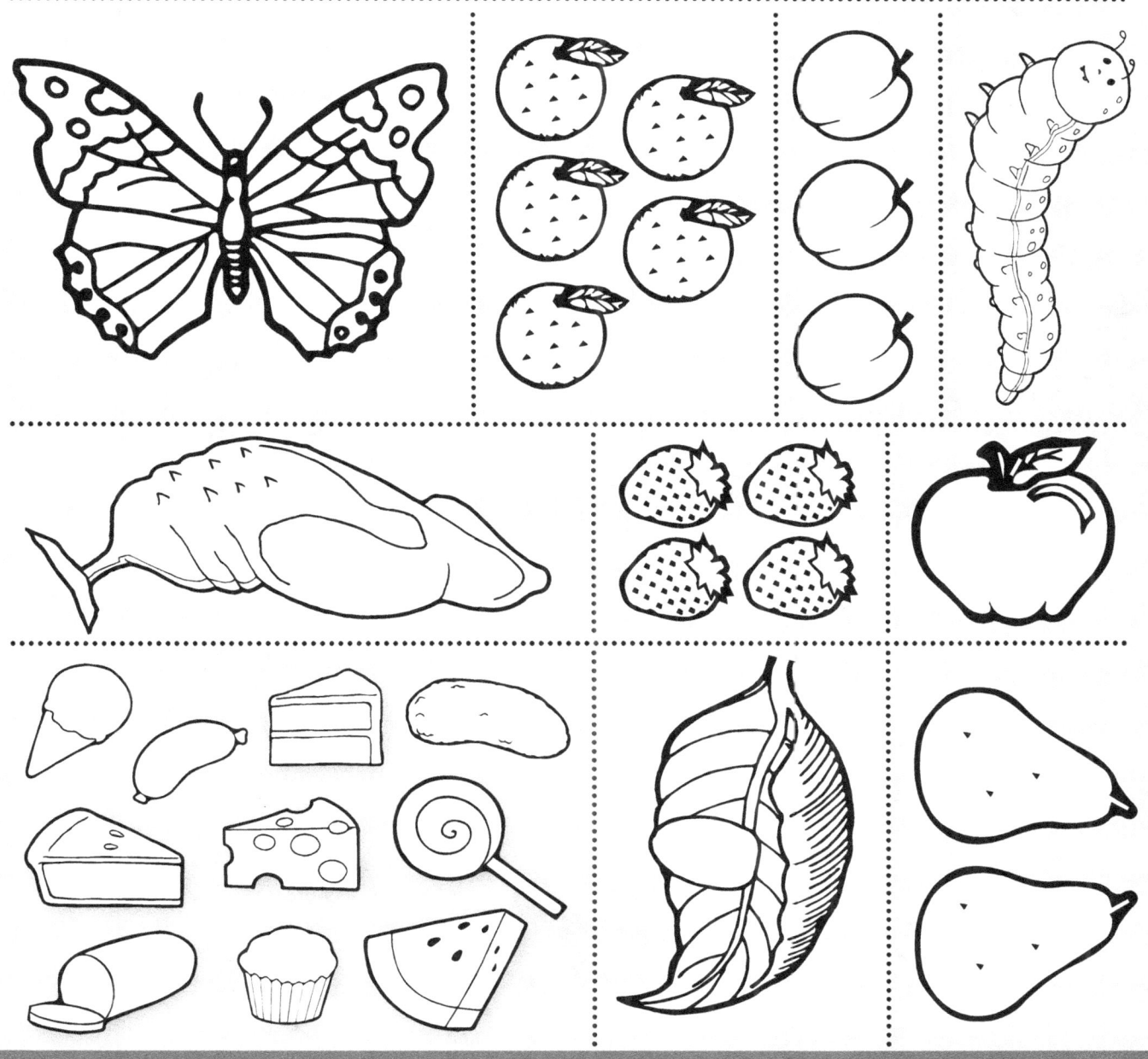

Learning Centre 4a

Level of Thinking: Analysing
Way of Learning: Bodily-Kinaesthetic

What am I?

- I am very small.
- I am stuck to a leaf.
- There are lots of us together.
- I am white or yellow.
- I have lots of legs.
- I like eating leaves.
- I grow bigger and bigger.
- I shed my skin.
- I hang off a branch.
- I am hard and shiny.
- Something is changing inside me.
- I have two wings.
- I have six legs.
- I have a head, a thorax and an abdomen.

Figure 31a

Learning Centre 4b

The Caterpillar (Larva)

Figure 31b

Learning Centre 4c

The Pupa (Chrysalis)

Figure 31c

Learning Centre 4d

Figure 31d

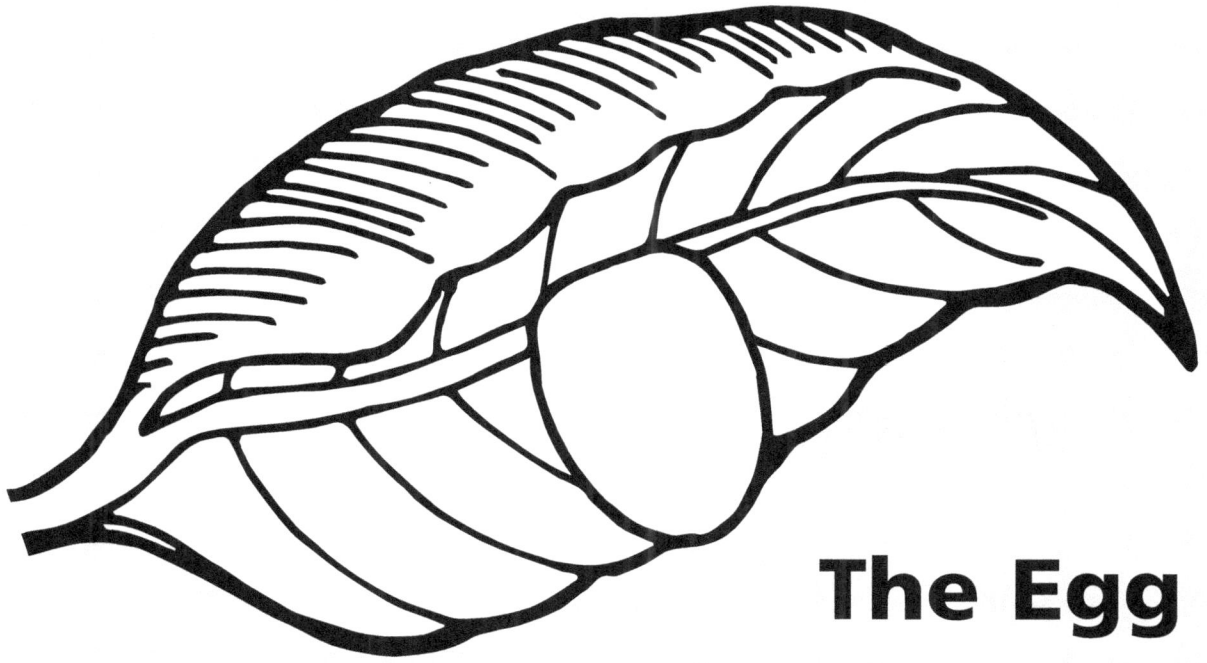

The Egg

Learning Centre 5

Level of Thinking: Analysing
Way of Learning: Visual-Spatial

Construct a Venn diagram:

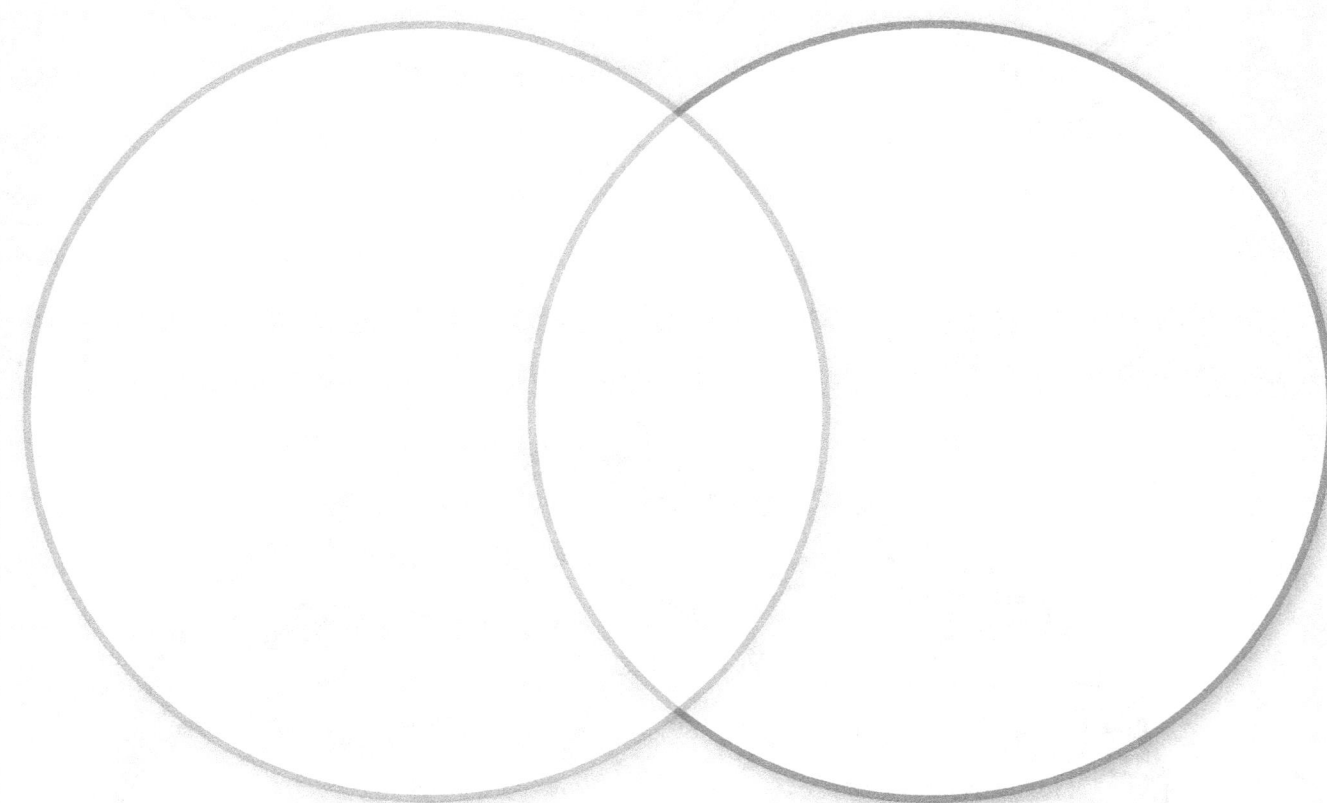

My needs　　　Needs of a butterfly

Figure 32

Marketing Your Boat – Year 9 science class

This Year 9 science unit was implemented in a large comprehensive high school in Brisbane. The unit 'Marketing Your Boat' has been used as the basis to create the eight corresponding Learning Centres (see Figure 33).

One of the strengths of units based on the matrix is that many of the activities can easily be adapted to create various Learning Centres. For example, Activity 8 (Verbal/Knowing) asks students to brainstorm all the different types of boats. If the teacher thought that this was a good Knowing activity, then why not reconstruct it so it can also be included in the Verbal Learning Centre? The heading of the activity remains the same, however, the students now need a list of thinking tools that may be useful for brainstorming purposes. One of the cornerstones of developing Learning Centres is providing additional information to the students.

The teacher then decided to restructure Activity 8 and provide their students with some additional information. Suggestions for thinking tools that might help students brainstorm included concept maps, Thinking clouds and TAP (Thinking All Possibilities).

Activities 8, 25, 27, 28, the RAT, 58 and 59 were reconstructed from the original activities found in the matrix. By adapting material that was already available, the teacher is working smarter, not harder, saving a huge amount of time. These activity cards can be found on pages 80–83.

It should be emphasised that the aforementioned activities make up only the Verbal Learning Centre. The teacher then chose activities from all the other multiple intelligences, creating eight different Learning Centres, namely Mathematical, Visual/Spatial, Kinaesthetic, Musical, Interpersonal, Intrapersonal and Naturalist. A huge amount of space would have been required if we covered activities from all Learning Centres, thus in this book we have chosen only to focus on those from the Verbal Learning Centre.

There are a number of different ways that the students can access these eight Learning Centres including:

- Placing the activities as A3, coloured, laminated posters on eight different tables, with each table representing one area of intelligence.
- Making the eight different Learning Centres available on a USB so students can download them on their personal computers.
- Downloading the eight Learning Centres on the computers held in the classroom, computer room or library.

The 48 Grid Planning Matrix - Marketing Your Boat (1 of 2)

Year Level: 9

Bloom's Taxonomy: Thinking Levels

Multiple Intelligences	Knowing	Understanding	Applying	Analysing	Creating	Evaluating
VERBAL I enjoy reading, writing and speaking	8. Brainstorm all the different types of boats. 24. What are the different ways that you can sell a product? **Thinking clouds**	25. Explain different ways that you can employ to sell a product. 26. Describe one of your favourite ads. Why is it effective?	49. Prepare the necessary ads, brochures, videos, web pages, public presentations, media releases and feature stories. **BROW**	28. Analyse the best way to market your boat. 27. Compare and contrast the best and the worst ad that you have seen.	**Real Assessment Task** Create a report, video, website or computer program titled 'Marketing your Boat'.	58. Assess your report/video/website/computer program. **LDC** 59. Present your Project to your class and receive feedback.
MATHEMATICAL I enjoy working with numbers and science	10. Review issues dealing with measurements and place value. 3. State what we mean by floating and sinking.	1. Use **PSDR** to predict what will happen to various fruits and vegetables when placed in water. 4. How will you float a potato in the centre of the bucket without using any strings or weights? **WINCE**	20. How much will you have to sell your boat for to make a profit? **TREC RedMast** 2. Carry out the learning activity 'Why do some objects float and others sink?' (See Appendix 2.) **PSDR**	5. Identify the issues that you had to deal with in floating the potato in the centre of the bucket? **TAP**	19. Estimate the cost of building your boat by including materials, labour and advertising. **TREC RedMast**	7. Evaluate the **PSDR** method and **WINCE** strategy. Were these thinking tools of any value to you in solving these problems? 6. Justify why your boat floated in the pool but not in the small tank.
VISUAL/SPATIAL I enjoy painting, drawing and visualising	9. Look at images of various boats. 29. Locate various menus that can be used on your boat.	13. Draw your own model boat. 30. Outline the various menus that will be available on your boat.	16. Choose the designs and paints for your boat. 31. Illustrate your menus. **W Chart**	32. Use the **Venn diagram** to compare two very different boats/menus.	17. Investigate the best way to paint the boat in order to prevent it from rusting. **TAP**	18. Assess your final shape and colours of your boat. Discuss ways to improve the shape and the colours.
KINAESTHETIC I enjoy doing hands-on activities, sports and dance	33. Find out what types of sports can be played on a boat.	34. Describe the main activities and sports that can take place on board a boat.	35. Show how one of these activities and sports are played. 14. Build or reassemble your boat.	36. Categorise these activities and sports in terms of their value to senior passengers.	52. Identify the issues dealing with environmental health, safety, food requirements, fitness and sports.	56. Were your passengers satisfied with the food, activities and sports that were available to them? How do you know?
MUSICAL I enjoy making and listening to music	37. Name the type of music and entertainment that is usually available to passengers on boats.	38. Match the type of music and entertainment to people of different ages.	39. Choose the music and entertainment that will be available to passengers on your boat.	40. Survey the type of music and entertainment that teenagers enjoy whilst on holidays. Will this music be suitable to older passengers?	41. Working with your group, compose a song, rap or dance. **LDC**	42. Present your song, rap or dance. Is it appropriate for teenagers? Suggest improvements.

Continued...

The 48 Grid Planning Matrix - Marketing Your Boat (2 of 2)

Year Level: 9

Bloom's Taxonomy: Thinking Levels

Multiple Intelligences	Knowing	Understanding	Applying	Analysing	Creating	Evaluating
INTERPERSONAL I enjoy working with others	11. Review basic rules of working with others.	12. How are the different roles going to be assigned? Who will decide?	23. Working as a group, commence your marketing plan.	50. How well did you work as a group? Survey every member of your group. **TPSS**	51. Are your passengers satisfied with the food, customer service and activities provided? Devise a survey.	53. Evaluate the impact that your boat is likely to have on the environment. **The Rake**
INTRAPERSONAL I enjoy working by myself	21. How do you feel when you are on board a boat? **LDC**	22. Express how you are feeling while on a boat in very rough seas. **Y Chart**	15. Share with another student your excitement when your boat actually floated.	55. Investigate your life as a boat builder.	54. Impersonate your favourite captain. **X Chart**	57. Carry out a **SOWC** analysis on the possible success of your boat business.
NATURALIST I enjoy caring for plants and animals	43. List all the items that you will need to take on board such as binoculars, running shoes, mosquito repellent, sunscreen, lotion, hat and suitable clothing.	44. Draw and/or photograph plants, animals and scenic sites whilst the boat is moving from one location to another and during the time that you are allowed on land.	45. Organise your own portfolio where you will keep your written observations, drawings, collections and photographs.	46. Select books, videos, CDs, films and nature simulations programs that will be available on board. On what basis will you select this material?	47. Create a map indicating nature walks, bird sites, rock formations, mountains, beach areas and tourist attractions that are located near the various places visited by the boat.	48. How difficult are these areas of interest for people of different ages and mobility? Are they accessible to people on wheelchairs? Rate them and recommend changes if necessary.

(This matrix was devised by Ralph Pirozzo in 1997 & updated in 2004)

Figure 33

Activity 8

Brainstorm all the different types of boats

Level of Thinking: Knowing

Which thinking tools would help you to brainstorm?

Suggestions
Concept Maps
Thinking clouds
TAP

Figure 34

Activity 25

Explain different ways that you can employ to sell a product.

Level of Thinking: Understanding

1. When buying things such as soft drinks, shoes, clothes, CDs and food, what are the **things that matter to you**?

2. Does the packaging, colours, texture and pictures have a **significant impact** on you?

Figure 35

Activity 27

Compare and contrast the best and the worst ad that you have seen.

Level of Thinking: Analysing

1. Use the **Venn diagram** to **compare and contrast** the best and the worst ad that you have seen.

2. Based on the **Venn diagram**, clearly state the **similarities and differences** between these two ads.

3. Now, you are ready to **prepare your own ad**!

Figure 36

Activity 28

Analyse the best way to market your boat.

Level of Thinking: Analysing

1. **Share your ideas** about the ways that you could market your boat with your group or class and receive their feedback using the **LDC**.

2. After you have received their feedback, how will you **incorporate their comments** into your marketing campaign?

Figure 37

RAT

Create your own report, video, website or computer program titled 'Marketing Your Boat'

Level of Thinking: **Creating**

❶ Is your product **new and unique?**

❷ If not, how can you use your **Higher Order Thinking Skills** to make it so?

See The Learning and Teaching Wheel.

Figure 38

Activity 58

Assess your report, video, website or computer program

Level of Thinking: **Evaluating**

❶ **Self-assess** your report, video, website or computer program using the **LDC**.

❷ **Encourage your group or class** to assess your report, video, website or computer program by using the **LDC**.

❸ Will this feedback enable you to **improve your product?**

Figure 39

> **Activity 59**
>
> **Present your project to your group, class or teacher and receive their feedback**
>
> Level of Thinking: **Evaluating**
>
> 1. Use a rubric to receive your **group, class or teacher's feedback.**
> 2. Advise how this rubric **can be improved.**
> 3. Was the feedback received based on this rubric **useful to you?** Will it enable you to improve your Project?
>
> Figure 40

Reflection

Much like Pip Riordan and Ros Mangold, teachers of the unit based on *The Very Hungry Caterpillar*, I found that the Year 9 students greatly enjoyed completing the Learning Centres. In particular, the amount of on-task behaviour increased significantly, and even though the students could complete the Learning Centres individually, often students were seen working in small groups. The students regularly produced work that was truly new and unique, and the quality of the work far exceeded that which these students normally produce when taught through more traditional methods.

If teachers want to improve their students' academic results, encourage independent learning and develop highly motivated students, then Learning Centres would have to be considered a very effective teaching strategy. However, if Learning Centres are such a wonderful idea, then one might wonder why don't we see them operating in every primary and secondary classroom? The reasons may include:

- Learning Centres require teachers to devote a good deal of time in finding the materials required for each Learning Centre to operate effectively and efficiently. Once they are established, however, the teacher only needs to slightly alter them to suit the needs of different students. As mentioned previously, this is

where units based on the matrix become very useful, because they provide the teacher with a significant number of activities that can be easily reconstructed.
- Some teachers, particularly in high school, have opted not to embrace Learning Centres due to the lack of space available in their classrooms. While this would have been a big limitation in the past, the advent of computers has solved this issue. These days, students can access and complete the activities contained in the various Learning Centres on their own computers, the IWBs located in the regular classroom and the computers in the computer room/library.
- The hustle and bustle often associated with the traditional Learning Centre is seen by some as chaotic, uncontrollable and unproductive. Devoting time to teaching students to work well in groups can prevent this. Teaching students to work cooperatively is covered in Chapter 2, Cooperative Learning Teams.
- There will often be a small number of students for whom Learning Centres will not work. This group may consist of autistic children and highly intrapersonal students who are unable to concentrate if there is too much noise in the classroom. To maximise these students' learning, the teacher should explore the implementation of other teaching strategies such as Learning Contracts and Individual Learning Plans.

References

Baker, B 2013, *Music learning centres: A resource for primary and early childhood classrooms*, School of Education, University of Tasmania.

Barrett, M 1996, *Learning centres in Music Education*, Uniprint, Launceston, Tasmania.

Carle, E 2009, *The Very Hungry Caterpillar*, Penguin Books, London.

Copple, C & Bredekamp S 2006, *Basics of developmentally appropriate practice: An introduction for teachers of children 3 to 6*, NAEYC, Washington, DC.

Epstein, AS 2007, *The intentional teacher: Choosing the best strategies for young children's learning*, NAEYC, Washington, DC.

Gardner, H 1983, *Frames of Mind*, Fontana Press, London.

Stuber, GM 2007, 'Centering your classroom: Setting the stage for engaged learners', *Beyond the Journal: Young Children on the Web*, NAEYC, Washington, DC.

Chapter 5
Multi-age Grouping

Like myself, many of you may have grown up in single-graded classrooms, thereby assuming that this system is both natural and universal. This is not the case, and as Pratt (1986) pointed out, it is neither geographically nor historically universal. For example, in 1985 a quarter of Scotland's primary schools had fewer than 50 students, 80 per cent of Portuguese children went to schools with no more than two classes and there were 11 000 one-teacher rural schools in France (Marshall 1985).

In Ontario, the Ministry of Education's published data indicates that in 2013 a total of 358 elementary schools were classified as very small schools (as reported by People for Education 2005).

Data published by the New South Wales Department of Education and Communities shows that in 2013 there were 571 small primary schools in rural and remote areas with teaching principals, 472 primary schools with fewer than 100 students and 127 schools with fewer than 20 students (New South Wales Department of Education and Communities 2013). Understandably, in these small schools there aren't enough students to create single-grade classes.

The history of Multi-age Grouping and single-grade classrooms

Studies of primates show that almost all of the living species of monkeys and apes grow up in societies characterised by diversity of age. According to Jolly (1972, p. 261), "the striking characteristic of young, socially living primates is their social play". In fact, the context in which the young primate moves from dependence on the mother to adulthood is the mixed-age play group.

A similar pattern exists in humans, according to anthropological studies. With approximately 180 hunter/gatherer societies still in existence today, such as the traditional Canadian Inuit, the Australian Aborigines and the !Kung San people (or Bushmen) of the Kalahari desert, we find that typically, these societies live in groups of 30–40 people, where the infant joins the play group after about the age of 18 months, imitating and relying on older children who take responsibility for the younger ones.

Cross-cultural studies have shown that in simpler societies, children spend more time looking after infants and are more nurturing than in more complex cultures. In all societies, aggression is more frequent among age-mates than in mixed groups (Whiting & Whiting 1975). So it's some wonder how we have moved from the mixed-age classroom of our early ancestors to the single-grade classroom that seems to be so prevalent in large primary and secondary schools in many countries today.

The age-stratified culture in which we live today is a product of the last two hundred years. In medieval Europe and in colonial America, children grew up surrounded by people of all different ages. Families were larger and classrooms contained considerable age diversity (Pratt 1986). In the dedicated one-room schoolhouse that emerged in the eighteenth century, a teacher would use individual and tutorial methods to instruct a group of 10 to 30 pupils ranging in age from 6 to 14 years (Cremin 1961).

The roots of the multi-age classroom come from the one-room schoolhouse in the United States. Prior to the school reforms of the 1830s and 1840s, multi-age education was the norm throughout the USA (Goodlad & Anderson 1987).

As reported by Cubblerly (1970), the death-knell of the one-room schoolhouse in the USA was sounded when Horace Mann, Secretary of Massachusetts Board of Education visited Prussia in 1843 and was impressed by the graded system operating in that country (Hallion, 1994). In his report titled *Seventh report to the Massachusetts Board of Education*, Mann stated that:

> The first element of superiority in a Prussian school consists in the proper classification of the scholars. In all places where the numbers are sufficient to allow it, the children are divided according to ages and attainment, and a single teacher has the charge only of a single class. There is no obstacle whatsoever to the introduction at once of this mode of dividing and classifying scholars in all our large towns (Cubblerly 1970, p. 84).

Within a decade of Mann's report to the Massachusetts Board of Education, the relevant legislation was passed in order to standardise age of entry, to establish sequential grade levels and to develop the appropriate curriculum. Of much interest is that school administrators widely accepted his proposal. This was the beginning of graded education in the USA, where children of the same age were grouped homogeneously. The birth of graded education developed simultaneously with America's industrial revolution and the massive immigration that followed during the mid-nineteenth century (Konner 1975).

Using the organisational structure of the factory as a model, children were grouped by age to make the delivery of education cost effective and time efficient. While this economy of scale reduced the cost of educating, it also meant that children were being tracked and labelled by finer and finer delineations of ability.

In fact, in Lowell's School Committee Report of 1852 it was reported that "the principle of the division of labor holds good in schools, as in mechanical industry. One might as justly demand that all operations of carding, spinning and weaving be carried out in the same room, by the same hands, as insist that children of different ages and attainments should go to the same school and be instructed by the same teacher". This was presented in the Lowell School Committee Report of 1852, as reported by Bruck (1970).

As expected, as the number of new industries boomed, more and more workers were needed to run these factories, thereby concentrating millions of people into cities. This population growth, plus the improved transportation systems that were needed to move the raw material, the finished products and the workers, facilitated the development of large comprehensive schools.

A return to the concept of multi-age classrooms did not receive much attention until 1959 with the publication of Goodlad and Anderson's book, *The Nongraded Elementary School*. The intent of this model was to move education beyond the lockstep standardised curriculum methods previously employed and by shifting the goal of instructional planning from the needs of the group to the needs of the individual child (McClellan & Kinsey 1999).

In the 1960s, many schools embraced the principles of non-graded education, partly due to the philosophy advocated by Goodlad and Anderson, and in response to a societal move from conformity to one that emphasised individuality. Coincidentally, multi-age programs peaked in the USA in 1990, the same year that saw the Kentucky Education Reform Act establish a state-wide, ungraded primary program that emphasised the delivery of multi-age and multi-ability learning experiences for all primary students in that state.

Regretfully, in recent years, some schools in the USA have discontinued their multi-age programs due to grade-level standards, testing requirements imposed by the No Child Left Behind Act and most states' accountability laws. These laws require students to take standardised tests by year level and by blurring the year-level standards, multi-age classrooms make this difficult. For example, in 1999 the Michigan Department of Education ceased state funding for multi-age programs on the basis that they are not compatible with year-level content and annual testing (Song, Spradlin & Plucker 2009, p. 6). These researchers point out that although the number of multi-age classrooms in the USA has declined, many educators continue to embrace the multi-age philosophy.

In addition, multi-age classrooms continue to operate in rural areas of Australia, Canada, Europe, New Zealand and many other parts of the world, because this strategy allows schools to operate more efficiently in staffing when class size cannot support one teacher per year level (Gutierrez & Slavin 1992).

Research regarding the advantages and disadvantages of Multi-age Grouping

Multi-age Grouping has and continues to be surrounded by controversy. For example, a major point of contention is whether Multi-age Grouping increases children's academic skills, and so far the results are inconsistent (Song, Spradlin & Plucker 2009).

While some of the studies regard Multi-age Grouping as beneficial, others show it having a negative impact on students' academic growth, and then there are others who indicate that it produces neither positive or negative results.

Veenman's (1995) review of 56 studies conducted in 12 countries concluded that there is not a significant difference in the quality of instruction between multi-age and single-grade classes. However, in a critique of Veenman's conclusions, Mason and Burns (1996) argued that instruction in multi-age classes was less effective since the multi-age classes usually had higher achievers and more experienced teachers.

Furthermore, Russell, Rowe and Hill (1998) examined the effect of multi-grade classrooms on student achievement in literacy and numeracy. This report was based on data from the Victorian Quality Schools Project, a large, comprehensive, three-year longitudinal study of school and teacher effectiveness in that state. Their analyses showed some significant negative effects on achievement associated with multigrade classes.

In July of 1997, the Minister for Education and Training in New South Wales (NSW) requested that a working group be formed to look at a range of multi-age classes in NSW primary schools. This working group reported that "Most schools in NSW form multi-age classes because either the total number or the spread of students within schools have compelled them to do so. The majority of schools large enough to form homogeneous classes based on age would have preferred to do so. The reasons given included:

- composites were unpopular with parents
- teachers preferred straight-age classes
- students preferred to be with their peers
- there was a perception that the workload was less with straight-age classes (pp. 13–14)

However, this report concluded that "Multi-age classes are a necessary pattern of organisation in many government and non-government schools across NSW and Australia, especially in rural areas. They will continue to be a significant proportion of classes in NSW schools (p. 23).

In contrast to Veenman's conclusions, findings of research studies in North America are beginning to indicate that Multi-age Grouping, when implemented as a philosophy of education, provides educational and social benefits. For example, Miller (1990) reviewed twenty one quantitative studies comparing the effects of multi-grade with single-grade classrooms and found that:

- the data clearly supports the multi-age classroom as a viable and equally effective organisational alternative to single-grade instruction
- regarding the affective domain, multi-grade students outperformed single grade students in over 75 per cent of the measures used

Anderson and Pavan (1993) reviewed 64 research studies and demonstrated improvement in test scores on standardised tests, and improved attitudes toward school for students in multi-age classes, especially for underachievers and students from a low socioeconomic background.

A major review examined the evidence bearing on the possible merits of multi-age classrooms, carried out in Canada by Pratt in 1986. In summarising the findings of experimental research and relevant evidence from ethology, anthropology and history, Pratt concluded, "The weight of this evidence strongly suggests that multi-age classrooms have many benefits to children which cannot be as fully realised in age-segregated classrooms" (p. 111).

Perhaps the most significant benefits to children in a multi-age environment are the social effects. For example, Goularte (1995) showed that students in multi-age classrooms developed positive attitudes about school and improved social skills. Another powerful reason why some teachers, principals and parents support the implementation of multi-age classrooms is because it's thought to engender feelings of belonging, emotional growth and nurturing in their classrooms.

It should be pointed out that for teachers who are passionate about the multi-age experience, no amount of adverse test results is going to deter them from lobbying and supporting its implementation. These highly committed educators value the idea that multi-age education recognises the natural development of the child. In fact, it places the child squarely at the centre of education. Privately, many have severe doubts about the capacity of present-day testing to actually capture the essence of the multi-age experience.

The Montessori Method (Montessori 1949) and Reggio Children (Edwards, Gandini & Forman 1998) also share the idea of fostering the natural development of the child, while placing them at the centre of education. Both The Montessori Method and Reggio Children have their own distinctive characteristics that have made them famous all over the world.

Perceived advantages of the ideal multi-age classroom

- The child comes first and multi-age education recognises the natural development of the child. The cornerstone of multi-age education is respect for the individual.
- It is child-centred, not curriculum-centred. A curriculum is offered that respects the child's interests, abilities, learning rates and styles.
- Teachers are constantly developing programs to suit the students instead of trying to fit the children to a prescribed set of outcomes. They choose the curriculum based on children's interests and needs.

- Children stay with the same teacher for three years, providing uninterrupted learning, strong relationships and increased continuity in planning.
- Children are not expected to perform at their age level, but encouraged to perform to the best of their abilities.
- Children learn from each other, so constructing knowledge takes place within a social context, rather than in isolation.
- Younger children benefit from the positive models of older students by aspiring to their levels of capabilities.
- Older students develop leadership skills by mentoring younger learners.
- Children have ample opportunities for modelling and imitations.
- Play is viewed as an important learning context for children because it enables them to construct their knowledge of the world by testing ideas, discovering relationships, abstracting information, expressing feelings and developing peer relationships.
- Classrooms become a family-like unit where each student is respected and supported.
- Better relationships are created among students, teachers and parents.
- No retention, promotion or labelling occurs.
- A strong focus is placed on success and authentic assessment.

(Gaustad 1992; Stone 2004)

Perceived disadvantages of the ideal multi-age classroom

- Russell, Rowe and Hill (1998) comment that there is strong support to the conclusions drawn from research that the multi-grade class structure is a more difficult, complex and challenging than that provided by the single-grade structure.
- The strongest, best and most experienced teachers are usually assigned to multi-age classes, thus 'robbing' the other students of this talent.
- Some parents of young children feel their sons or daughters may be overwhelmed by the older students.
- Some parents of older students feel their sons or daughters will spend all their time tutoring the younger students and will not learn anything new.
- Some parents, teachers and principals argue strongly that children of different grades are too diverse in ability to be effectively educated in the same classroom.
- Some parents of gifted students or children with learning difficulties feel these learners will be neglected.
- Parents with a high income who are involved with school life tend to promote Multi-age Grouping, so there's potential for these groups to be full of privileged and affluent children. This homogeneity doesn't align with the multi-age philosophy of heterogeneity.

- Some administrators and senior officers of the Department of Education oppose them because they are not compatible with grade-level content and annual testing.
- If a child develops a negative relationship with other students and/or the teacher, this will be exacerbated by the fact that they will be spending a possible three years in this classroom.

How should the ideal multi-age classroom be defined for research purposes?

Lloyd (1999) stressed that it's difficult for researchers to generalise the academic impact of multi-age education due to the wide range of ways multi-age groups are implemented. Veenman (1995) pointed out that the prevailing confusion about multi-age education might be due to its inconsistent definition. For example, researchers and practitioners use many labels to describe multi-age education including: multigrade, multi-age, mixed-age, composite, double grade, spilt grade and vertical grouping. Thalheimer (2010) argues that these terms are often confusing and redundant, making research difficult.

Given the confusion that surrounds this area, I propose the following as a working definition for a multi-age classroom:

A multi-age classroom refers to the deliberate placing of children of different ages, abilities and genders in the same classroom with the same teacher for a minimum of three years (e.g. F–2). Each age group should be randomly selected to ensure a balance in relation to age, gender and ability.

Furthermore, Stone (2004) emphasised that the groups should be deliberately made for the benefit of children, not for reasons of economics, curriculum or convenience. The groupings should evolve into a true family of learners.

Multi-age Grouping is designed to increase the heterogeneity of the group, thus capitalising on the different experiences, knowledge and abilities of children. The current system of grouping students according to their birthday is challenging, as it's based on the assumption that students of the same age are ready to learn the same material at the same rate and in the same amount of time.

At the end of this review, it becomes clear that three different types of multi-age classrooms can exist.

1. Classrooms where the ideal model is fully utilised for pure pedagogical reasons. These schools tend to be located in large towns and cities and have the ability to randomly select and balance the class with children based on age, ability and gender. In future, given the present demands on schools for year-level content and annual testing, one would predict that these would be few in number.
2. Classrooms where some parts of the ideal model is utilised for pedagogical reasons, and because the number of children attending is too small to form straight-age classes. These should be referred to hybrid multi-age classes.

3. Classrooms where no part of the ideal model is utilised, with the exception that, due to logistical reasons, a group of students of different year levels are placed in the same class with the same teacher. These should not be referred to as multi-age classrooms, rather, they should be referred to as composite classes.

It stands to reason that future research studies should be confined to ideal multi-age classrooms only. Moreover, whatever testing needs to be done for research purposes should occur during the third year of its operation so the accumulative effect of the multi-age experience may be detected and measured.

For teachers in remote rural areas, multi-age teaching is not an experiment or a new educational trend, but a reality dictated by the school's financial concerns and location. A rural school with 20 children is unlikely to have more than one teacher appointed, something that's unlikely to change any time soon. Fundamentally, these teachers do not have or are likely to ever have the luxury of implementing the ideal multi-age model, given the fact that by law they have to enrol the students living in their towns and surrounding farms.

Teachers in small schools have two choices. One is to treat this class as a composite, and implement no part of the ideal multi-age model. It follows that these teachers will be educating these students as if they were discrete year levels. The other is to treat the class as a hybrid multi-age class, thus implementing parts of the ideal multi-age model.

Given that I do considerable work in rural schools, I support the implementation of the hybrid multi-age model, though I am aware that it isn't perfect. At times in education, one has to be both a pragmatist and a realist for the betterment of the children. It is undoubtedly better for children to have access to the hybrid model than being taught as discrete year levels.

Implementing Multi-age Grouping

The school in question is located in a small rural town with 980 inhabitants and is situated 60 km from the next town. The latter has a population of 5800 people, is 521 km from the state's capital city and serves as the agricultural centre for a large area.

The school's enrolment consists of 43 students from F–7, and the classes are formed as follows:

- The F–2 class has 15 children and is taught by a very experienced teacher.
- The Year 3–5 class has 18 children and is taught by a first-year teacher that has just been transferred to this school following the retirement of a well-regarded and experienced teacher.
- The Year 6–7 class has 11 children and is taught by the principal.
- The teaching principal has responsibilities that include teaching the Year 6–7 class, acting as the support teacher and teacher librarian. He is also required to:
    - oversee the implementation of the relevant curriculum and all the year level testing as mandated by the employing authorities

- supervise the teaching and non-teaching personnel
- implement all the relevant policies (such as privacy, child protection, health and safety, anti bullying, gifted and talented and children requiring special assistance)
- organise the playground duties roster, weekly assemblies, speech nights, swimming carnivals and a yearly trip to Parliament House
- manage the allocated funds, build strong relationships with the Parents and Citizens Association and the local community
- prepare and submit the annual school report

Based on a formula dictated by the total number of students enrolled, these are the entitlements:

- The principal is entitled one day per week for office and administration duties.
- The other two teachers receive two hours each per week for planning.
- To enable the principal and the two teachers to access this non-teaching time, a local supply teacher is employed.
- The school is entitled to a school administrative manager five days per fortnight and a general assistant for eight hours a week.

I've been invited to support the Year 3–5 teacher, who has been attempting to teach this class primarily by preparing work sheets aimed at each individual year level. These have had catastrophic consequences, such as:

- significant behavioural issues, particularly with the boys. Some of these boys have had to be suspended – a rather unusual occurrence for this small school
- regular complaints from the parents who are threatening to transfer their children to the other non-state school
- a significant number of days that this teacher has been absent due to illness. In the first three months, this teacher lost a significant amount of weight and has repeatedly approached the principal asking to be transferred to a regular school in the nearest capital city. Being a state-run school, this is completely beyond the capacity of the principal. As an integral part of their employment, teachers are required to accumulate a certain number of points working in rural and disadvantaged schools prior to being eligible for transfer to a bigger school

Doing nothing and allowing this teacher to flounder with this class is not an option, both for the children's sake and for this teacher's professional integrity. For this teacher to thrive in their multi-level classroom, differentiation may be the key. As discussed in the introduction, it's essential for teachers who are going to differentiate their classrooms to know their students. The data needed should include the students' reading ages, mathematics scores, preferred multiple intelligences and interests.

Fortunately, most of the formal information needed was already available in the students' personal profiles, compiled by the previous teacher. This teacher was extremely keen on gathering 'hard' data on their students and then using this data as the basis for differentiation.

This data revealed that these Year 3–5 students:

- display reading ages ranging from Year 1 to Year 8 (a commercially available reading test was used)
- display a wide range of mathematical abilities (a commercially available maths test was used)
- scored very high in the visual, kinaesthetic and interpersonal learning styles. This information tells the teacher that, on the main, these students will be most engaged when presented with visual material such as: posters, using the IWB, the Internet, and YouTube. They also showed engagement in hands-on activities and when working cooperatively with others students

By speaking to the principal, other teachers and some parents, I gathered informal data showing that:

- since the beginning of the year, an increased level of teasing, pushing and shoving and bullying has been witnessed both in the classroom and in the playground
- there has been a strong disapproval of the way this teacher handled the classroom, which is significantly different to the way the last teacher worked
- On numerous occasions, parents have complained that their children are coming home saying they are bored and do not want to school. Losing students when your total enrolment is only 43 is not an option

This information was tabulated in the 'Gathering Information for Differentiation' form as shown on page 7, and presented to this teacher who quickly realised that it would be most unproductive to continue teaching this Year 3–5 class as if it were to be made up of three separate groups, and to rely on students completing work designed for each individual year level.

Now that we had an in-depth knowledge of these students, we were ready for a strong planning framework. A framework that enables the teacher to engage these students by providing for their thinking skills, while engaging them through their preferred learning styles, using a combination of explicit teaching and choices so differentiation could take place.

As previously mentioned, teachers can create a strong planning framework by using the matrix template. This multi-level planning tool derives its strength and flexibility from blending together six of the world's best theories and taxonomies: Bloom's Taxonomy, Multiple Intelligences (Gardner), Backward Design (McTighe and Wiggins), The Spiral Curriculum (Bruner), Choices Theory (Glasser) and the Zone of Proximal Development (Vygotsky).

Given the fact that in this Year 3–5 classroom we had children with learning difficulties, disadvantaged learners, average students and gifted children, we decided to use The 56 grid matrix because it has the new level of thinking referred to as Pre-Knowing.

During term two at this school, students were to explore how they can stay healthy. The decision was made to create a unit titled 'Keeping Healthy'. In planning this unit, the '10

Steps to Creating Outstanding Units' (see page 23) were followed diligently.

This means commencing the unit-planning cycle by identifying the relevant descriptors as mandated by the hiring authority, exploring with the students what they would like to do to demonstrate their knowledge and generating a rubric for each of the Real Assessment Tasks (RATs). The RATs indicate the culminating activities that will be collected by the teacher for marking, assessment and reporting purposes and are coloured yellow (light grey in book).

Once teachers know what the students would like to create and how their products are going to be assessed, they are in a wonderful position to determine how they are going to support the students in their journey.

Based on the knowledge of the children obtained in the 'Gathering Information for Differentiation' form, the decision was made to teach some of the activities to the entire class (the explicit teaching activities coloured in blue or dark grey) and other activities would be made available to the students as choices. The children then could choose to complete the choices by themselves, in cooperation with other students or by co-constructing with the teacher (these are the activities in white squares).

Then, a variety of thinking tools were selected and layered onto the matrix. These thinking tools were hyperlinked so that the teacher and the students could use them on the IWB (see Figure 41).

Furthermore, the scope and sequence as indicated by the number placed in front of each activity (with the exception of the activities listed in the Pre-Knowing column) was determined. These numbers provide the students with a guide on how they may choose to complete the various activities available to them. For example, one would expect that in order for the students to complete activity 43, 'Create your cooking sensation', they would have already completed activity 35, 36, 37, 38, 39, 40, 41 and 42.

Throughout this unit, the teacher devoted a good deal of time to:
- introducing the critical learning to all the students, as indicated in the blue or dark grey activities
- modelling how to use the variety of thinking tools to be found in this unit
- demonstrating how to safely handle knives, a variety of foods and food scraps
- co-constructing with individual students and groups of students whenever necessary
- providing feedback and reflecting with students on a regular basis and at the end of activity 15, 21, 32, 43 and 48
- reviewing the basic structure on how to best work in groups and how to provide effective feedback
- ensuring that students' presentations and reflections as represented by activity 10, 16, 22, 28, 34, 44 and 49 ran smoothly, on time and that all students paid attention to the group presenting their products, so they could provide them with their feedback based on the LDC (see page 39)

- reflecting on how to further improve this unit, for example, asking students to graph their family's expenditure on food based on the five food groups, providing students with more choices in RAT 3 and 4 and advising them not to place meat scraps in their bins, composts and small gardens)

- In order to establish this hybrid multi-age classroom, the teacher decided to establish three groups:
    - Group 1: Year 3 (6 students)
    - Group 2: Year 4 (6 students)
    - Group 3: Year 5 (5 students)

The teacher proceeded to teach the explicit material to all students (blue or dark grey activities under Pre-Knowing), then devoted the rest of the time in co-constructing, providing feedback and reflecting with the various groups. Of critical importance is the fact that this learning and teaching strategy enabled students to move up and down within the various groups. For example, a student in Group 3 having difficulties in maths can join Group 2 while this group is reviewing basic maths skills. Simultaneously, a bright Year 1 student who excels in writing may join Group 3 while they are involved in a creative writing session.

The 56 Grid Planning Matrix - Keeping Healthy (1 of 3)

Year Level: 3/4/5

Bloom's Taxonomy: Thinking Levels

Multiple Intelligences	Pre-Knowing	Knowing	Understanding	Applying	Analysing	Creating	Evaluating
VERBAL I enjoy reading, writing and speaking	Teacher introduces/reviews the value of surveys. Teacher reflects with the students at the end of activity 32 to check for understanding.	29. Research what surveys are used for (surveys help us to collect information from people).	30. Brainstorm using the **Thinking clouds** how surveys can be conducted (over the telephone, mail, emails, text messages and in person).	31. Prepare a survey to find out the types of foods eaten by children at your school. (If some students were to find this activity too difficult, then they will be provided with a teacher pro forma.)	**Real Assessment Task 1** 32. Carry out your survey. **Group 1:** survey your group **Group 2:** survey your class **Group 3:** survey your entire school	33. Construct a summary of the surveys. What do they tell us? Do children at your school have a balanced diet? Obtain a copy of your school canteen's menu and study it in detail. (Group work)	34. Recommend how your school's canteen menu could be improved so that children at your school will be eating more healthy foods. Present your suggestions to your group/teacher/canteen worker.
MATHEMATICAL I enjoy working with numbers and science	Teacher introduces/reviews: • **Thinking clouds** eating disorders such as anorexia, bulimia and obesity • the available data that links child obesity to an increased risk in developing Type 2 diabetes. TREC Teacher reflects with the students at the end of activity 46 and 48 to check for understanding.	1. Why do we eat? Brainstorm using the **Thinking clouds** and have a class discussion.	2. Based on the **Thinking clouds** and class discussion in Activity 1, explain to your group why we need to eat. 45. Estimate how much your family spends on food in one day (this should include all the foods bought such as milk, bread, eggs, cheese, meat, fish, vegetables and fruit). Discuss these costs with your parents/guardians.	3. What would happen to students of your age if they decide to stop eating? 46. Calculate how much your family spends on food. **Group 1:** one day **Group 2:** one week **Group 3:** one month TREC	4. Research the main eating disorders that could impact on teenagers and prepare a table indicating the eating disorder, its cause, its impact and what can be done about it. 47. Show your calculations to your group or teacher and receive their feedback.	**Real Assessment Tasks 2** 48. Based on your group or teacher's feedback carry out your final calculations. **Group 1:** one day **Group 2:** one week **Group 3:** one month	49. Present your final calculations to your class and place your results on the classroom wall so that other students can view them. Bring a copy of your final calculations home. Show them to your parents/guardians and receive their feedback. How accurate was your estimate?

continued...

The 56 Grid Planning Matrix - Keeping Healthy (2 of 3)

Year Level: 3/4/5

Bloom's Taxonomy: Thinking Levels

Multiple Intelligences	Pre-Knowing	Knowing	Understanding	Applying	Analysing	Creating	Evaluating
VISUAL/SPATIAL I enjoy painting, drawing and visualising	Teacher introduces/reviews: • Access to YouTube • Venn diagrams • Healthy and non-healthy foods • The five food groups **LDC** Teacher reflects with the students at the end of Activity 15 to check for understanding.	11. Locate pictures of all kinds of foods in newspapers, brochures, magazines and YouTube.	12. Separate these two groups into healthy and unhealthy using a **T Bar**.	13. On what basis did you decide what foods are healthy and non-healthy? Now, compare your list with the information provided on the Five Food Groups.	14. Compare and contrast healthy and non-healthy foods using a Venn diagram.	**Real Assessment Task 3** 15. Encourage children at your school to eat more healthy foods by creating a: Group 1: poster Group 2: collage Group 3: PowerPoint presentation	16. Present your poster, collage and PowerPoint presentation to your class or school. **LDC** Record your presentation on video.
KINAESTHETIC I enjoy doing hands-on activities, sports and dance	Teacher introduces/reviews: • The fact that we need energy in order to live (e.g. running, swimming, walking). This energy comes from the foods we eat. • Basic functions of the respiratory and circulatory systems.	5. Students are shown how to take their pulse while resting and after they have walked or run for five minutes.	6. Why is your pulse faster after you have exercised? Explain.	7. Examine what happened whilst you were walking/running for five minutes. Did your breathing rate also increase? Why?	8. Investigate how much physical exercise you should do per day/week. Present your draft to your group/teacher for comments and suggestions.	9. As a group, design a daily or weekly exercise plan.	10. Assess and recommend changes to your daily or weekly plan to make sure that it is appropriate for you. How will you know?
MUSICAL I enjoy making and listening to music	Teacher introduces/reviews **LEAP**.	23. List 10 songs, jingles or ads that have food themes.	24. Select one of these songs, jingles or ads and explain their message.	25. Using basic instruments found in the music room, make a song/jingle/ad encouraging children to eat healthy foods. **LEAP**	26. Analyse your song, jingle or ad by playing it to your group or teacher and receive their feedback based on **LDC**.	27. Based on your group/teacher's feedback, create your final song, jingle or ad as a group.	28. Present your final song, jingle or ad to your class, parade or other classes. With permission from your teacher, video your final presentation and place it on the school's website.

Continued...

The 56 Grid Planning Matrix - Keeping Healthy (3 of 3)

Year Level: 3/4/5

Bloom's Taxonomy: Thinking Levels

Multiple Intelligences	Pre-Knowing	Knowing	Understanding	Applying	Analysing	Creating	Evaluating
INTERPERSONAL I enjoy working with others	Teacher introduces/reviews: • A balanced diet • T bar Teacher introduces/reviews health and safety issues when handling sharp/butter knives. (Send a letter to parents regarding allergies) Teacher reflects with the students at the end of Activity 43 to check for understanding.	35. Group discussion relating to healthy and non-healthy foods. List 10 healthy foods and 10 unhealthy foods. 36. What impact will this information have on your diet?	37. Share this information with your group/class/parents/grandparents/guardians. 38. List all the foods that you eat in a day. Complete a T bar of healthy and unhealthy foods.	39. Based on this list, explain to another student/group whether or not your diet is balanced. TPS 40. Students and teacher discuss the foods needed for their cooking sensation and again review health and safety issues.	41. Analyse your list and state clearly which foods you will keep on your list and which foods you will try to reduce or avoid. 42. Students ensure that their area is clean and tidy and that they have organised all the food needed for their cooking sensation.	**Real Assessment Task 4** 43. Create your cooking sensation using the W Chart: Group 1: sandwich Group 2: milkshake Group 3: pizza/fruit salad/fried rice	44. Share your cooking sensation with your class. Did they enjoy it? Assess whether or not you included the foods required for an active teenager? Suggest how you can improve your cooking sensation.
INTRAPERSONAL I enjoy working by myself							
NATURALIST I enjoy caring for plants and animals	Teacher introduces/reviews health and safety issues when handling food scraps. Check OHS laws relevant to your state or territory. Teacher reflects with the students at the end of activity 21 to check for understanding.	17. What happens to all the food that is not eaten by students at your school?	18. Carry out a brainstorming activity and then outline what students can do with all the food scraps.	19. Prepare a plan to build a bin, compost or small garden to use all the food scraps produced by the canteen, students and staff.	20. Investigate the best place for your bin, compost or organic garden to be located. Consult the grounds person.	**Real Assessment Task 5** 21. Create the following: Group 1: bin Group 2: compost Group 3: small garden	22. Evaluate how effective your bin, compost or organic garden has been in discarding all the food scraps. Advise how you will reduce the bad smells produced by your bin, compost or small garden.

(This matrix was devised by Ralph Pirozzo in 1997 & updated in 2004)

Figure 41

Reflection

- At the completion of this unit, the teacher, principal and parents were delighted with the students' change in behaviour, commitment to completing the RATs and the quality of work produced.
- Student engagement was extremely high throughout this unit and one of the most pleasing aspects of this classroom was to see children joining different groups depending on the focus of the activity. For example, on a regular basis children with learning difficulties in Group 3 worked with Group 2 during their maths calculations; bright children in Group 2 joined Group 3 while the latter were working on designing, administering and summarising the results of their surveys; Group 2 and 3 helped children in Group 1 getting ready for their various presentations and Group 1, 2 and 3 children worked together in celebrating their cooking sensations with their parents in the local park. A fundamental assumption of multi-age classrooms is that children of different ages support each other's learning.
- The teacher regularly and deliberately involved the parents in various activities, including helping their sons or daughters to carry out surveys, calculate how much their family spends on food and provide the necessary materials for the children to create their cooking sensations. Upon creating these cooking sensations, parents joined the children in celebrating by having lunch at the local park. Parents commented how much they enjoyed seeing their children performing their jingle or ads.
- The teacher is no longer approaching the principal asking to be transferred to another school, students are no longer being suspended and parents are no longer threatening to move their children to the other non-government school.
- Whether this means that all issues have been solved depends on whether or not this teacher continues to operate the classroom as a hybrid multi-age classroom. Things may be very different if the teacher were to return to treating this Year 3–5 class as three separate groups, and to rely mainly on work sheets designed for each year level.
- While this class by no means represents the ideal model of a multi-age classroom, it represents the beginning of a hybrid model.
- As previously mentioned, this unit can be improved by providing children with many more choices to complete their RATs and many more thinking tools. In future, one would anticipate that this teacher would implement additional teaching strategies such as Learning Contracts for gifted and talented children, as well as Learning Centres and Individual Learning Plans for children with learning difficulties.

It becomes clear that, when placed in these multi-level classrooms, teacher training, preparation and adequate support is the key if they are to take advantage of these heterogeneous grouping strategies.

The willingness to adjust one's teaching methodology so markedly in such a short period of time is truly refreshing. This young, inexperienced teacher should be congratulated for being so receptive to the suggestions made, thereby significantly altering the way the curriculum is now being delivered in this classroom.

References

Anderson, RH & Pavan BN 1993, *Nongradedness: Helping it to happen*, Technomic Publishing, Lancaster, PA.

Bruck D 1970, 'The schools of Lowell, 1824–1861: A case study in the origins of modern public education in America', doctoral dissertation, Harvard University.

Edwards, C, Bandini L & Forman G 1998, *The Hundred Languages of Children: The Reggio Emilia Approach – Advanced Reflections*, 2nd edn, Ablex Publishing Corporation, Westport, CT.

Cubberley 1970, *Readings in public education in the United States*, Greenwood Press, Westport, CT, pp. 287–288.

Gaustad, J 1992, Non-graded Primary Education, *ERIC Digest*, no. 74, ED347637, <http://files.eric.ed.gov/fulltext/ED347637.pdf>.

Goodlad, JI & Anderson RH 1987, *The Nongraded Elementary School*, Teachers College Press, New York, NY.

Goularte, R 1995, *Multi-Age Classrooms*, National Education Association, Washington, DC.

Gutierrez, R & Slavin R 1992, *Achievement effects of the non-graded elementary school: A retrospective review*, Centre for Research on Effective Schooling for Disabled Students, John Hopkins University, Baltimore, MD.

Hallion, AM, 1994, 'Strategies for developing multi-age classrooms', paper presented at the annual convention of the National Association of Elementary School Principals Association in 1994, Orlando, FL.

Jolly, A 1972, *The Evolution of Primate Behaviour*, Macmillan, New York, NY.

Konner, M 1975, 'Relations among infants and juvenile in comparative perspectives', in M Lewis & LA Rosenblum (eds), *Friendship and peer relations*, Wiley, New York, NY.

Mariano, LT and Kirby SN 2009, 'Achievement of Students in Multigrade Classrooms: Evidence from the Los Angeles Unified School District', RAND Education, <www.rand.org/content/dam/rand/pubs/working_papers/2009/RAND_WR685.pdf>.

Marshall, DG 1985, 'Closing small schools: Or when is small too small?', *Education Canada*, vol. 25, no. 3, pp. 10–16.

Mason, DA & Burns, RB 1996, '"Simply no worse, and simply no better" may simply be wrong: A critique of Veenman's conclusions about multigrade classes', *Review of Educational Research*, no. 66, pp. 307–322.

McClellan, DE & Kinsey, SJ 1999, 'Children's social behaviour in relation to participation in mixed-age or same-age classrooms', *Early Childhood Research and Practice*, vol. 1, no. 1, <http://ecrp.uiuc.edu/v1n1/mcclellan.html>.

Miller, BA 1990, 'A review of the quantitative research on multiage instruction', *Research in Rural Education*, vol. 7, no. 10, pp. 1–8.

Montessori, M 1949, *The Absorbent Mind*, Theosophical Publishing House, Madras, India.

New South Wales Department of Education and Training 1997, *Multi-Age Classes in New South Wales*, curriculum directorate, <http://www.schools.nsw.edu.au/media/downloads/schoolsweb/studentsupport/programs/classsize/multiage/multi_age.pdf>.

New South Wales Department of Education and Communities 2013, *Rural and Remote Education: A Blueprint for Action*. New South Wales Government, viewed December 4, 2013, <https://www.det.nsw.edu.au/media/downloads/about-us/our-reforms/rural-and-remote-education/randr-blueprint.pdf>.

People for Education 2005, *Ontario's Small Schools*, Ontario Ministry of Education, Ontario, viewed January 9 2014, <http://www.peopleforeducation.ca/wp-content/uploads/2011/07/Ontarios-Small-Schools-2005.pdf>.

Pratt, DP 1986, 'On the Merits of Multiage Classrooms', *Research in Rural Education*, vol. 3, no. 3, pp. 111–115.

Russell, VJ, Rowe, KJ & Hill, PW 1998, 'Effects of Multigrade Classes on Student Progress in Literacy and Numeracy: Quantitative Evidence and Perceptions of Teachers and School Leaders', paper presented at the Annual Conference of the Australian Association for Research in Education in 1998, Adelaide, South Australia.

Stone, S 2004, *Creating the Multiage Classroom*, 2nd ed, Good Year Books, Tucson, AZ.

Thalheimer, W 2010, *K–12 Classrooms: Research review of multigrade, multiage, combination classrooms*, Will at Work Learning, <http:/www.willatworklearning.com/2010/11/multiage-classrooms1.html>.

Veenman, S 1995, 'Cognitive and Non-cognitive Effects of Multi-grade and Multi-age Classes: A Best Evidence Synthesis', *Review of Educational Research*, vol. 65, no. 4, pp. 319–381.

Whiting, BB & Whiting JWM 1975, *Children of six cultures: A psychocultural analysis*, Harvard University Press, Cambridge, MA.

Chapter 6
Individual Learning Plans

An Individual Learning Plan is a written curriculum document that allows a student to select the most appropriate pathway to complete the Real Assessment Task (RAT) within a specified amount of time. This takes advantage of the student's preferred learning styles in order to maximise their learning potential. The classroom teacher should construct this, in cooperation with the student and with other teaching and non-teaching personnel such as teacher assistants, enrichment teachers, guidance officers and parents.

Individual Learning Plans should be made available to students who are underachieving, and may also work well for students who have not responded well to other forms of differentiation.

In this section we will endeavour to show how a unit based on the matrix can be reconstructed to generate Individual Learning Plans for:

- students with learning difficulties, EAL/D learners and disadvantaged children
- average students
- gifted and talented students
- students with significant behavioural issues

We will concentrate our efforts on students with learning difficulties growing in an economically disadvantaged household. However, the same approach can be used to cater to the needs of EAL/D (English as an Additional Language or Dialect) students.

If teachers are going to cater for the needs of students with learning difficulties, it's essential that they define who these students are. This is where we quickly run into trouble because there's no single definition for students with learning difficulties. Every state, territory and even every country has its own definition.

However, for the purpose of this book we will embrace a working definition proposed by the Queensland Studies Authority that refers to learning difficulties as "barriers that limit access to, participation in, and outcomes from the curriculum" (2007, p. 1). In Queensland, students with learning difficulties are those whose access to the curriculum is limited because of short-term or persistent problems with literacy, numeracy or learning how to learn.

These students have learning difficulties due to a combination of at least three factors:

1. Weaknesses in processing, decoding and encoding.
2. Undeveloped learning-how-to-learn skills.
3. Being taught with inappropriate effective learning and teaching strategies.

To some extent, the above definition shares some similarities to the one advanced by Westwood (2008, p. 2) who points out that "learning difficulties may be the result of a specific learning disability, but they are much more likely to be due to environmental factors such as social disadvantage, inappropriate curriculum, inadequate teaching or lack of positive support for learning".

The good news is that teachers can support students with learning difficulties in all the areas mentioned above, however, due to the focus of this book we will concentrate only on the implementation of Individual Learning Plans. Having said this, one would expect that the implementation of appropriate learning and teaching strategies will improve these students' processing, decoding and encoding skills and their learning-how-to-learn strategies.

Some of the characteristics associated with students with learning difficulties are:

- consistent reading and spelling errors
- avoiding reading aloud and writing assignments
- misreading information and not extracting useful information from reading material
- lack of effective learning strategies, resulting in persistent low achievement
- poor memory skills, leading to poor recall
- taking a long time to remember facts and learn new skills
- unable to concentrate for long periods
- easily bored and distracted, resulting in less time spent in active learning
- impulsive behaviour
- problems with conforming to acceptable codes of behaviour
- poor attitude and low self-esteem
- difficulty in planning and summarising
- trouble with open-ended questions on tests
- difficulties with time management and organisation
- lack of motivation when presented with material that doesn't interest them

While this list may be disheartening for teachers and parents of students with learning difficulties, there is still a great deal of hope. Teachers now can support these students with a variety of computer-based programs, by tapping into their preferred learning styles and by implementing various learning and teaching strategies. In fact, the opportunity to improve the education of students with learning difficulties has never been better.

Based on experience working with students with learning difficulties, I found that the primary area students require support is in reading, writing and basic maths skills. It is these reading difficulties that bring these students to the attention of teachers, who then refer them for various intervention programs.

The inability to read and extract meaning from written material has an overall negative impact on all academic subjects. According to Jenkins and O'Connor (2002), the inability to rapidly identify words actually impairs comprehension, because struggling readers devote more processing resources to identifying words, thus overloading their working memory. These students then have difficulty in storing, retrieving and applying this information.

In my previous role as head of remedial education (a term no longer in use), I never ceased to be amazed by the hidden talents of students with learning difficulties. I remember working with students that had been referred for some maths remediation because they had failed their recent maths test, only to find that they could answer all the questions correctly once they were read aloud. I'd work with a group of students who were referred because they were causing the teacher major behavioural problems when learning about the solar system through a teacher-directed mode – sitting down and copying notes from the blackboard or from the IWB. These students became highly engaged when asked to draw and build their own space station, even though they were relying on the same data that they previously tried to learn by note taking. Here, the power of learning styles is revealed in a most dramatic and practical way.

One of the most remarkable features of the theory of multiple intelligences is how it provides teachers with at least eight different potential pathways to engaging students. Thus, if a student is having difficulty in learning some material through the linguistic or logical way of instruction, teachers have at least another six different ways to present this material in order to facilitate learning.

For example, if a student were to have a highly developed visual-spatial intelligence, this tells the teacher that the student represents things spatially, tends to think in pictures and needs to create mental images to retain information. This information now enables the teacher to choose from many pathways for this student's developed visual-spatial intelligence. It's of great importance to teachers that they can use these strengths to help students overcome some of their weaknesses. This is exactly what happened to the students who became highly engaged in their learning when they were given the opportunity to draw and build their space station.

Implementing Individual Learning Plans

To better understand how Individual Learning Plans actually work in the real classroom, we will use the example of four students: Jeff, Melissa, Cheryl and Pat. These students are attending an integrated Year 9 class at a rural comprehensive high school, with their ages ranging from 14–15 years old. If needed, the classroom teacher has access to a teacher assistant and to the learning enrichment teacher. The unit being studied this term is titled 'Marketing Your Boat', a 10-week unit which sees the students devote 50 minutes per day to its completion.

Jeff

Jeff has been classified as a student with learning difficulties and is living in an economically disadvantaged family. This classification has been based on the data available in his 'Gathering Information for Differentiation' form, which shows:

- a reading age of 11, which is four years below his chronological age
- a score of 17 out of 42 on Promoting Learning International's Mathematics Diagnostic Test. This is very low score for a Year 9 student when considering that the average score on this test for Year 7 students is 28 with a standard deviation of 5
- his marks range from 30 to 40 per cent in almost all subjects
- his RAMP (representing his three preferred learning styles), consisting of visual, kinaesthetic and intrapersonal intelligences
- comments from teachers indicate that Jeff avoids participating in class discussion and doesn't appear to be interested in any of the subjects studied. His homeroom teacher confided that Jeff may be using this as a defence mechanism to avoid being humiliated from giving the wrong answers
- a note from the guidance officer states that Jeff's dad has left home and that currently there is no significant male figure in Jeff's life
- from an early age, his mother noticed that Jeff's speaking and reading skills were delayed compared to his two younger brothers and sister
- the family of four survives on welfare payments, given the fact that Jeff's father has moved to another state to take a low-paying job in the local grocery store. He refuses to financially support Jeff's family as he doesn't earn enough money to even feed himself, his new partner and her two children

Given that Jeff has not responded well to Ability Grouping, Cooperative Learning Teams, Learning Contracts, Learning Centres or Multi-age Grouping, the decision has been made to offer Jeff the opportunity to complete this unit through an Individual Learning Plan.

Traditionally, constructing an Individual Learning Plan takes anywhere between 10 and 15 hours. This is totally untenable given that this teacher has five classes with 30 students in each. On any given day, this teacher is responsible for the learning of 150 students, plus having to attend meetings, do playground duties and coach the school tennis team. If Individual Learning Plans are going to be a serious option for differentiation, then we must find a quicker way to construct them, otherwise they will not happen at all.

This is where the matrix becomes extremely useful as it enables teachers to take advantage of existing units to create the student's Individual Learning Plan. This should take no more than one hour. Given the huge amount of time previously needed, this seems unlikely, however, with the support of the classroom teacher, the teacher assistant and/or the learning enrichment teacher, all Jeff needs to do is to select the activities that he would like to do in order to achieve the Real Assessment Task.

Once Jeff has marked the activities that he would like to complete with a pencil or pen, the teacher quickly deletes the activities that Jeff has not selected (these are primarily in the Higher Order Thinking Skills) and adds a few activities in the Pre-Knowing level. With the advent of computers, this should not take more than one hour.

This approach is similar to what was suggested in the introduction, that students with learning difficulties should devote about 70 per cent of their time working in the Lower Order Thinking Skills (LOTS) and 30 per cent in the Higher Order Thinking Skills (HOTS). It is critical that we don't "dumb down" Jeff's curriculum.

Jeff, is still required to complete the RAT for marking, assessment and reporting purposes. Even though the RAT and its corresponding rubric have been modified, the demands of the learning have not changed. What *has* changed is the fact that Jeff now chooses the pathway to complete the RAT – one that takes advantage of his preferred learning styles. Given that Jeff has learning difficulties, he will receive additional support through the activities listed under Pre-Knowing.

Jeff's Individual Learning Plan can be found on page 112.

Melissa

Based on the data presented in her 'Gathering Information for Differentiation' form, Melissa has been classified as a student with average learning abilities. The data shows:

- a reading age of 14. This is in line with her chronological age
- a score of 25 out of 42 on Promoting Learning International's Mathematics Diagnostic Test. These results are slightly below average based on the average score on this test for year 7 students is 28 with a standard deviation of 5
- marks between 50 and 60 per cent in almost all subjects
- her RAMP (representing her three preferred learning styles) consists of verbal, musical and interpersonal intelligences
- teacher comments that, at present there is nothing remarkable about Melissa's academic results. However, they were very keen to emphasise the fact that Melissa is very gregarious, is very well liked by her classmates and is always willing to help the teachers and the other students. The teachers commented that Melissa spends the least amount of time in completing her assignments in order to have more time with her friends. There was an overwhelming agreement among her teachers that Melissa could do much better academically if she applied herself to her school work
- Melissa lives with her mother, father and a younger brother in an house that one would consider to be average for their neighbourhood

Similar to Jeff, Melissa has not responded well to Ability Grouping, Cooperative Learning Teams, Learning Contracts, Learning Centres or Multi-age Grouping. Thus, Melissa has been offered the opportunity to complete this unit through an Individual Learning Plan.

Once Melissa had perused the unit, 'Marketing Your Boat', with the help of the classroom teacher, the teacher assistant and/or the learning enrichment teacher, Melissa re-organised the order that she would like to complete the various activities (represented by the number next to each activity). Melissa's teacher was then able to generate a copy of this reconstructed unit in less than one hour. In doing so, Melissa has chosen her own route to success.

Based on the fact that Melissa has been classified as an average learner, the teacher felt that there was no need to include any activities in the Pre-Knowing level. As an average student, Melissa should spend equal amount of time working in LOTS and the HOTS.

Melissa's Individual Learning Plan can be found on page 114.

Cheryl

It is impossible not to notice Cheryl, as she is an extremely tall and thin girl wearing very thick glasses. Often Cheryl can be found sitting quietly in her seat, giving the impression that she would rather be somewhere else. She is failing all her subjects – not due to innate ability, but because she is unable to sit for the regular tests and exams. The teachers are at a loss on what to do about this once very gifted student.

A comparison between her 'Gathering Information for Differentiation' form and notes on her Year 7 personal file reveals a very different story.

- The file is full of comments like:
    - "uses words and expressions that are well above what one would expect from a Year 7 student"
    - "in my entire teaching career, I have never met anyone as bright as Cheryl"
    - "outstanding maths reasoning skills"
    - "great command of the English language"
    - "her science assignments are brilliant"
    - "an asset to have in my drama group"
    - "delighted that she is taking a leading role in this year's musical"
    - "one of the best netball players that this school has ever had"
    - "what a joy to see Cheryl mentoring students with learning difficulties"
- The Multiple Intelligence test completed in Year 7 produced very high scores in the Verbal, Mathematical and Intrapersonal intelligences.
- Achievement levels of over 95 per cent and above in all her Year 7 exams and her nation-wide testing placed her at the 95th percentile in literacy and numeracy.
- An only child, living with her parents who run the local takeaway store in town. The town is struggling financially due to the severe drought that has affected this area for the last three years. They have extremely high expectations for their daughter – since Cheryl was in Year 1 they have been telling everyone she will become a medical doctor.

At the beginning of Year 8, things started to change – Cheryl was resented by the other students who often whispered nasty things about her, and calling her names such as 'the professor'. She became the target of an unrelenting bullying campaign orchestrated by a group of jealous girls. This involved name-calling, stalking, spreading offending rumours and posting unflattering messages on various social networks.

The teacher, parents and the school's administration attempted to stop this bullying but all efforts failed, and it got worse. The parents considered moving their daughter to another school, but the nearest government school is over 100 km away and they cannot afford to send Cheryl to a boarding independent school in the nearest capital city.

Cheryl felt let down by her teachers, parents and the school and despaired that she had absolutely no control over this depressing situation. Sadly, this led her to develop a severe form of Anorexia Nervosa. This once very talented student now spends two days a week at the local hospital being fed through a nasal gastric tube. Her condition is being closely monitored by the local GP who regularly briefs the school on her progress.

Regardless of all the dreadful things that have happened to Cheryl, she still wants to do well at school and her dreams of becoming a medical doctor have not been dashed.

In Year 9, a note from the guidance officer states that Cheryl 'seems to fall apart' before and during any written exams. Any mention of tests brings an acute nervous attack culminating in vomiting and severe headaches. From what the guidance officer is saying, it seemed to me that Cheryl should be treated as a gifted underachiever. To an extremely busy high school teacher who is responsible for the learning of 150 students, what does this really mean, and most importantly, what can we do about it?

Cheryl's teacher wants to do the very best for her and is aware of the fact that Ability Grouping, Cooperative Learning Teams, Learning Centres and Multi-age Grouping would not work because of her regular absenteeism. Learning Contracts were considered, but not implemented in the event that Cheryl would react negatively towards the point system. The decision was made to offer Cheryl the opportunity to complete this unit through an Individual Learning Plan, because she could complete some of the activities while in hospital.

Once Cheryl had perused the original unit, in consultation with the classroom teacher and/or the learning enrichment teacher, Cheryl proceeded to mark all the activities that she would like to complete, and re-organised the order she wanted to complete them. This is represented by the number placed next to each activity.

Now, the teacher is able to devise Cheryl's Individual Learning Plan in less than one hour. This plan reflects the fact that Cheryl has chosen to spend about 30 per cent of her time working on LOTS and about 70 per cent working on HOTS. This is in line to what had been predicted for gifted and talented students in the introduction.

In doing so, Cheryl has carved her own route by choosing not to devote any time in activities listed under Knowing, because she already has an in-depth knowledge of this material. No teacher would want a gifted maths student to review issues dealing with measurement and place value, when this student has been placed in the 95th percentile in nation-wide numeracy testing. It's no wonder some of our brightest students get bored when we teach to the middle.

The plight of gifted underachievers has been well-documented by a large number of workers in the field of gifted education (Colangelo, Kaplan, Reis, Siegel and Coach, Van Tassel-Baska, Whitmore and others) and in my article published in *The Roeper Review* (Pirozzo, 1982).

Cheryl's Individual Learning Plan can be found on page 116.

Pat

The arrival of a troubled student can dramatically change the climate in one's classroom, and this is exactly what happened upon Pat's arrival. Pat arrived at this school with no pen, paper or textbooks. He did not wear the school's uniform and his jeans and shirts looked like they had just been put through the wringer. People like Pat were an uncommon occurrence at this school, and his behaviour was one that this teacher hoped would not become a trend, so the decision was made to investigate his situation further.

After talking with other teachers, it became clear that many of them were also having problems with Pat. For example, one of his teachers remarked, "he is a most argumentative, impulsive and defiant young man", and another commented, "He goes out of his way to interfere with other students' learning". Another claimed, "I have never seen anyone so rude, abrupt and with such a negative attitude in my thirty years of teaching".

Checking Pat's personal file revealed very little, as the referring independent college refused to share information, arguing that privacy laws prevented them from doing so. Similarly, there was no information on Pat's 'Gathering Information for Differentiation' form because no one had the time to create one.

The good news is that this comprehensive high school is located in a relatively small rural town, where everyone knows everyone, so it didn't take too long to discover that Pat's grandparents had managed an 8000-acre wheat property located about an hour's drive from town. Last year, upon the sale of this large property, they moved into town hoping for a quiet and relaxed retirement.

A quick call to his grandparents revealed that Pat's parents split up about two years ago and soon after that both his mum and dad moved in with their respective new partners. At first Pat went to live with his mother, which didn't last too long because he could not get along with his stepfather – a towering man with a sharp tongue and explosive temper. A six-month stay with his father proved to be a total disaster because his stepmother would "boss him around". At one time he was heard yelling out, "I would prefer to be in jail than staying in this place!" Pat was sent to his grandparents in the hope that they would be able to control him.

Back to the classroom, Pat would act obnoxious and make fun of everyone, including the teacher. At one stage he was seen rolling on the floor using his index finger as if it were a gun, shooting at the other students. In doing so, he has become the centre of attention, which is exactly what he'd hoped to do. This could not go on, as he is deliberately undermining the teacher's authority and preventing other students from learning. So what is the teacher to do?

Out of sheer frustration, the teacher sat down with Pat and provided him with a marker and a copy of the 'Marketing Your Boat' unit. The teacher gave him 10 minutes with the instruction to mark the activities he would like to do. Pat was thrilled that he was able to choose which activities he got to do for the next 10 weeks.

The teacher collected the pages that comprise this unit, and in no time was able to remove any activities he did not select. This Individual Learning Plan could also have been constructed by simply colouring in activities that Pat chose with a brightly-coloured marker.

With total amazement, we found Pat working through the activities as chosen by him. He was still responsible for completing the Real Assessment Task (RAT) and to hand this in by the due date for marking, assessment and reporting purposes. However, he happily completed the RAT, having chosen the activities himself.

One could speculate that a number of factors contributed to his sudden, positive change in behaviour. This includes one teacher who showed Pat a great deal of patience and understanding, who didn't send him to the office when many others would have done so, took the time to investigate why he was behaving so badly, and deliberately made contact with his grandparents. This was the teacher who trusted Pat in selecting his own learning route to complete the RAT.

Pat still continues to disrupt other classrooms where 'chalk and talk' or note taking is the preferred teaching style. As any large school would have it, there are only likely to be a few teachers who honestly believe they have to teach every single item to their students, and that they are the fund of all knowledge. For these types of teachers, the idea of providing students with choices is completely foreign. It will be interesting to discover how they will manage Pat's challenging behaviour – one would hope that they will eventually embrace different learning and teaching strategies to provide the most engaging and exciting learning environment to Pat and to all other students.

Pat's Individual Learning Plan can be found on page 118.

The 56 Grid Planning Matrix

LD, EAL/D and Disadvantaged Students – Individual Learning Plan (1 of 2)

Student: Jeff
Marketing Your Boat

Multiple Intelligences	Pre-Knowing	Knowing	Understanding	Applying	Analysing	Creating	Evaluating
VERBAL — I enjoy reading, writing and speaking	6. Teacher deals with the spelling of: • boat • boats • boating 45. Introduces/reviews **BROW**, **Concept maps** and **Thinking clouds**.	5. Brainstorm all the different types of boats. 46. What are the different ways that you can sell a product? **Thinking clouds**	47. Explain different ways that you can employ to sell a product. 48. Describe one of your favourite ads. Why is it effective?	51. Prepare the necessary ads, brochures, videos, web pages, public presentations, media releases and feature stories. **BROW**	49. Compare and contrast the best and the worst ad that you have seen.	**Real Assessment Task** Create a model, collage, report, video, website or computer program titled 'Marketing Your Boat'. (The RAT and the relevant rubric have been modified for this student.)	53. Present your Project to your class and receive feedback (use a criteria sheet).
MATHEMATICAL — I enjoy working with numbers and science	7. Teacher introduces/reviews words like: • floating • sinking • density 8. Teacher introduces/reviews the **PSDR Method**, **TREC** and **RedMast**.	43. Review issues dealing with measurements and place value. 11. State what we mean by floating and sinking.	9. Use the **PSDR** method to predict what will happen to the various fruits and vegetables when placed in water.	44. How much will you have to sell your boat to make a profit? **TREC** **RedMast** 10. Carry out the learning activity 'Why do some objects float and others sink?' (See Appendix 2.) **PSDR**			
VISUAL/SPATIAL — I enjoy painting, drawing and visualising	1. Teacher shows the children a variety of boat-related photographs and pictures. 17. Teacher introduces/reviews **TAP** and **W Chart**.	18. Locate various menus that can be used on your boat.	13. Draw your own model boat. 20. Outline the various menus that will be available on your boat.	15. Choose the designs and paints. 21. Illustrate your menus. **W Chart**	19. Use the Venn Diagram to compare two very different menus.	16. Investigate the best way to paint the boat in order to prevent it from rusting. **TAP**	
KINAESTHETIC — I enjoy doing hands-on activities, sports and dance	2. Teacher encourages students to look and touch a variety of models relating to boats.	22. Find out what types of activities and sports can take place on board a boat.	23. Describe the main activities and sports that can take place on board a boat.	14. Assemble your boat by following your own design. Work in cooperation with your team. 24. Show how one of these activities or sports are played.			

Continued...

Chapter 6 - Individual Learning Plans

The 56 Grid Planning Matrix
LD, EAL/D and Disadvantaged Students – Individual Learning Plan (2 of 2)

Student: Jeff **Marketing Your Boat**

| Multiple Intelligences | Pre-Knowing | Bloom's Taxonomy: Thinking Levels |||||
		Knowing	Understanding	Applying	Analysing	Creating	Evaluating
MUSICAL I enjoy making and listening to music	3. Teacher plays music relating to boating and fishing.	29. Name the type of music that is usually available to passengers on board boats.	30. Match the type of music and entertainment to people of different ages.	31. Choose the music and entertainment that will be available to passengers on your boat.		32. Working with your group, compose a song, rap or dance. **LDC**	33. Present your song, rap or dance. Is it appropriate for teenagers? Recommend improvements.
INTERPERSONAL I enjoy working with others	26. What do we mean by working with others? 25. Introduce or review **TPS** and **TPSS**.	27. Review basic rules of working with others.	28. How are the different roles going to be assigned? Who will decide?	50. Working as a group, commence your marketing plan.	52. How well did you work as a team? Survey every member of your group. **TPSS**		
INTRAPERSONAL I enjoy working by myself	4. The teacher asks students to imagine that they are on a boat. 34. Introduces **LDC** and **X and Y Charts**.	35. How do you feel when you are on board a boat? **LDC**	36. Express how you feel while on a boat in very rough seas. **Y Chart**	37. Share with another student your excitement when your boat actually floated.	38. Investigate your life as a boat builder.	39. Impersonate your favourite captain. **X Chart**	
NATURALIST I enjoy caring for plants and animals	12. The teacher asks the students what types of material could be used to build a boat?	40. List all the items that you will need to take on board such as binoculars, running shoes, mosquito repellent, sunscreen lotion, hat and suitable clothing.	41. Draw and/or photograph plants, animals and scenic sites while the boat is moving from one location to another and during the time that you are allowed on land.	42. Organise your own portfolio where you will keep your written observations, drawings, collections and photographs.			

Content descriptions/learning outcomes/the essential learnings: _____

Resources: _____

Figure 42

The 56 Grid Planning Matrix
The Average Student – Individual Learning Plan (1 of 2)

Student: Melissa **Marketing Your Boat**

Bloom's Taxonomy: Thinking Levels

Multiple Intelligences	Pre-Knowing	Knowing	Understanding	Applying	Analysing	Creating	Evaluating
VERBAL I enjoy reading, writing and speaking		2. Brainstorm all the different types of boats.	29. Use **Thinking clouds** to explore different ways that you can sell a product.	30. Prepare the necessary ads, brochures, videos, web pages, public presentations, media releases and feature stories. **BROW**	31. Compare and contrast the best and the worst ad that you have seen.	**Real Assessment Task** Create a report, video, website or computer program titled 'Marketing Your Boat'.	47. Present your Project to your class and receive feedback (use a criteria sheet).
MATHEMATICAL I enjoy working with numbers and science		32. Review issues dealing with measurements and place value.	3. Use the **PSDR** method to predict what will happen to the various fruits and vegetables when placed in water (see Appendix 2).	4. Carry out the learning activity 'Why do some objects float and others sink?' (See Appendix 2.) **PSDR**	33. Investigate how much you will have to sell your boat in order to make a profit.	34. Estimate the cost of building your boat by including materials, labour and advertising. **TREC RedMast**	35. Could you have built the boat using different materials?
VISUAL/SPATIAL I enjoy painting, drawing and visualising		1. Look at pictures of various boats.	5. Draw your own model boat and show it to your teacher.	6. Choose the designs and paints for your boat.	7. Apply the first coat of paint to your boat. Are you satisfied with the finished product? How could you improve it?	8. Investigate the best way to paint the boat in order to prevent it from rusting. **TAP**	9. Assess your final shape and colours of your boat. Discuss ways to improve the shape and the colours.
KINAESTHETIC I enjoy doing hands-on activities, sports and dance		10. Find out what types of activities and sports passengers can do/play on board a boat.	11. Describe the main activities and sports that can be done/played on board a boat.	12. Build or reassemble your boat.	13. Categorise these activities and sports in terms of their value to senior passengers.	42. Identify the issues dealing with environmental health, safety, food requirements, fitness and sports.	43. Were your passengers satisfied with the food, activities and sports that was available to them? How do you know?
MUSICAL I enjoy making and listening to music		14. Name the type of music and entertainment that is usually available to passengers on board boats.	15. Match the type of music and entertainment to people of different ages.	16. Choose the music and entertainment that will be available to passengers on your boat.	17. Survey the type of music and entertainment that teenagers enjoy whilst on holidays. Will this music be suitable to older passengers?	18. Working with your group, compose a song, rap or dance. **LDC**	19. Present your song, rap, dance. Is it appropriate for teenagers? Recommend improvements.

Continued...

Chapter 6 - Individual Learning Plans

The 56 Grid Planning Matrix
The Average Student – Individual Learning Plan (2 of 2)

Student: Melissa **Marketing Your Boat**

Bloom's Taxonomy: Thinking Levels

Multiple Intelligences	Pre-Knowing	Knowing	Understanding	Applying	Analysing	Creating	Evaluating
INTERPERSONAL I enjoy working with others		20. Review basic rules of working with others.	21. How are the different roles going to be assigned? Who will decide?	22. Working as a group, now commence your marketing plan.	23. How well did you work as a group? Survey every member of your group. **TPSS**	44. Are your passengers satisfied with the food, customer service and activities? Devise a survey.	45. Evaluate the impact that your boat is likely to have on the environment. **The Rake**
INTRAPERSONAL I enjoy working by myself		24. How do you feel when you are on board a boat? **LDC**	25. Express your feelings while on a boat in very rough seas. **Y Chart**	26. Were you excited when your boat actually floated? **TPS**	27. Investigate your life as a boat builder.	28. Impersonate your favourite captain. **X Chart**	46. Is your boat building business likely to succeed?
NATURALIST I enjoy caring for plants and animals		36. List all the items that you will need to take on board.	37. Draw and/or photograph plants, animals and scenic sites whilst the boat is moving from one location to another.	38. Organise your own portfolio where you will keep your written observations, drawings, collections and photographs.	39. Select books, videos, CDs, films and nature simulations programs that will be available on board.	40. Create a map indicating nature walks, bird sites, rock formations, mountains, beach areas and tourist attractions that are located near the various places visited by the boat.	41. How difficult are these areas of interest for people of different ages and mobility?

Content descriptions/learning outcomes/the essential learnings: _____

Resources: _____

Figure 43

The 56 Grid Planning Matrix
The Gifted and Talented Student – Individual Learning Plan (1 of 2)

Student: Cheryl **Marketing Your Boat**

Bloom's Taxonomy: Thinking Levels

Multiple Intelligences	Pre-Knowing	Knowing	Understanding	Applying	Analysing	Creating	Evaluating
VERBAL I enjoy reading, writing and speaking			11. Explain different ways you can employ to sell a product.	40. Prepare the necessary ads, brochures, videos, web pages, public presentations, media releases and feature stories. **BROW**	13. Analyse the best way to market your boat. 12. Compare and contrast the best and the worst ad that you have seen.	**Real Assessment Task** Create a report, video, website or computer program titled 'Marketing Your Boat'.	41. Assess your report, video, website or computer program. **LDC** 42. Present your Project to your class and receive feedback (use a criteria sheet).
MATHEMATICAL I enjoy working with numbers and science			1. Predict what will happen to the various fruits and vegetables when placed in water. **PSDR** 3. How will you float a potato in the centre of the bucket without using any strings or weights? **WINCE**	2. Carry out the learning activity 'Why do some objects float and others sink?' (See Appendix 2.) **PSDR**.	4. Identify any major issues that you had to deal with in floating the potato in the centre of the bucket. **TAP**	14. Estimate the cost of building your boat by including materials, labour and advertising. **TREC RedMast**	6. Evaluate the **PSDR** method and **WINCE** strategy. Were these thinking tools of any value to you in solving these problems? 5. Justify why your boat floated in the pool but not in the small tank.
VISUAL/SPATIAL I enjoy painting, drawing and visualising			7. Draw your own model boat.	8. Choose the designs and paints for your boat. 18. Illustrate your menus. **W Chart**	17. Use the **Venn diagram** to compare two very different boats/menus.	10. Investigate the best way to paint the boat in order to prevent it from rusting. **TAP**	9. Assess your final shape and colours of your boat. Discuss ways to improve the shape and the colours.
KINAESTHETIC I enjoy doing hands-on activities, sports and dance			15. Describe the main activities and sports that can be played on board a boat.	14. Build or reassemble your boat.	16. Categorise these activities and sports in terms of their value to senior passengers.	23. Identify any issues surrounding environmental health, safety, food requirements, fitness and sports.	32. Were your passengers satisfied with the food, activities and sports that were available to them? How do you know?

Continued...

The 56 Grid Planning Matrix
The Gifted and Talented Student - Individual Learning Plan (2 of 2)

Student: Cheryl   **Marketing Your Boat**

Bloom's Taxonomy: Thinking Levels

Multiple Intelligences	Pre-Knowing	Knowing	Understanding	Applying	Analysing	Creating	Evaluating
MUSICAL I enjoy making and listening to music				19. Choose the music and entertainment that will be available to passengers on your boat.	20. Survey the type of music or entertainment that teenagers enjoy whilst on holidays. Will this music be suitable to older passengers?	21. Working with your group, compose a song, rap or dance. **LDC**	22. Present your song, rap or dance. Is it appropriate for teenagers? Recommend improvements.
INTERPERSONAL I enjoy working with others			24. How are the different roles going to be assigned? Who will decide?	39. Working as a group, commence your marketing plan.	30. How well did you work as a group. Survey your group. **TPSS**	31. Are your passengers satisfied with the food, service or activities? Devise a survey.	33. Evaluate the impact that your boat is likely to have on the environment. **The Rake**
INTRAPERSONAL I enjoy working by myself			25. Express your feelings while on a boat in very rough seas. **Y Chart**	26. Were you excited when your boat actually floated? **TPS**	27. Investigate your life as a boat builder.	28. Impersonate your favourite captain. **X Chart**	29. Carry out a **SOWC** analysis on the possible success of your boat business.
NATURALIST I enjoy caring for plants and animals			34. Draw and/or photograph plants, animals and scenic sites while the boat is moving from one location to another and during the time that you are allowed on land.	35. Organise your own portfolio where you will keep your written observations, drawings, collections and photographs.	36. Select books, videos, CDs, films and nature simulations programs that will be available on board. On what basis will you select this material?	37. Create a map indicating nature walks, bird sites, rock formations, mountains, beach areas and tourist attractions that are located near the various places visited by the boat.	38. How difficult are these areas of interest for people of different ages and mobility? Are they accessible to people on wheelchairs? Rate them and then recommend changes if necessary.

Content descriptions/learning outcomes/the essential learnings: _____

Resources: _____

Figure 44

The Student with Challenging Behaviour – Individual Learning Plan (1 of 2)

The 48 Grid Planning Matrix

Student: Pat **Marketing Your Boat**

Bloom's Taxonomy: Thinking Levels

Multiple Intelligences	Knowing	Understanding	Applying	Analysing	Creating	Evaluating
VERBAL — I enjoy reading, writing and speaking	2. Brainstorm all the different types of boats. 19. What are the different ways that you can sell a product? **Thinking clouds**	20. Explain different ways that you can employ to sell a product. 21. Describe one of your favourite ads. Why is it effective?	24. Prepare the necessary ads, brochures, videos, public presentations, media releases and features. **BROW** 25. Show your draft to your teacher and make suggested improvements.	22. Analyse the best way to market your boat. 23. Compare and contrast the best and the worst ad that you have seen.	**Real Assessment Task** 26. Create a report, video, website or computer program titled 'Marketing Your Boat'.	27. Assess your report, video, website or computer program. **LDC** 28. Present your project to your class and receive feedback (use a rubric).
MATHEMATICAL — I enjoy working with numbers and science		3. Use the **PSDR** method to predict what will happen to the various fruits and vegetables when placed in water (see Appendix 2.)	4. Carry out the learning activity 'Why do some objects float and others sink?'. (See Appendix 2.) **PSDR**			
VISUAL/SPATIAL — I enjoy painting, drawing and visualising	1. Look at various boats.	5. Draw your own model boat.	6. Choose the designs and paints for your boat.	10. Apply the first coat of paint to your boat.	7. Investigate the best way to paint the boat in order to prevent it from rusting. **TAP**	8. Assess the final shape and colours of your boat. Discuss ways to improve the shape and the colours.
KINAESTHETIC — I enjoy doing hands-on activities, sports and dance	11. Find out what types of activities and sports can take place on board a boat.	12. Describe the main activities and sports that can take place on board a boat.	9. Build or reassemble your boat.	13. Categorise these activities and sports in terms of their value to senior passengers.		

Continued...

Chapter 6 - Individual Learning Plans

The 48 Grid Planning Matrix
The Student with Challenging Behaviour – Individual Learning Plan (2 of 2)

Student: Pat
Marketing Your Boat

Multiple Intelligences	Bloom's Taxonomy: Thinking Levels					
	Knowing	Understanding	Applying	Analysing	Creating	Evaluating
MUSICAL I enjoy making and listening to music	14. Name the type of music and entertainment that is usually available to passengers on board boats.			15. Survey the type of music that teenagers enjoy whilst on holidays. Will this music be suitable to older passengers?	16. Compose a song, rap or dance. LDC	7. Present your song, rap or dance. Is it appropriate for teenagers? Recommend improvements.
INTERPERSONAL I enjoy working with others						
INTRAPERSONAL I enjoy working by myself			18. Commence your marketing plan.			
NATURALIST I enjoy caring for plants and animals						

Content descriptions/learning outcomes/the essential learnings: _____

Resources: _____

Figure 45

Reflection

It should be stressed that the terms used to describe Jeff, Melissa, Cheryl and Pat (i.e. students with learning difficulties, average students, gifted underachievers and students with challenging behaviour) are to some extent arbitrary, based on both hard data and subjective means. While this is not a perfect system, the only way to undermine this concern would be to have these students to do an IQ test. Many teachers are unable to find the financial means to carry out this type of testing, and we can't place too much faith in its reliability and predictability when testing disadvantaged students with learning difficulties, gifted underachievers and troubled youths.

With the exception of Pat, the 'Gathering Information for Differentiation' form was found to be extremely useful in gathering both formal and informal information, enabling teachers to get to know their students. This data is crucial if teachers are serious about differentiating the curriculum.

As stated previously, the construction of Individual Learning Plans normally takes 10 to 15 hours. This is not an option for very busy teachers, which is why the matrix provides them with a realistic alternative, because they can develop an Individual Learning Plan in less than an hour by reconstructing existing units.

In completing these Individual Learning Plans, the students' learning has not been 'dumbed down' as they are still expected to complete the Real Assessment Tasks (RATs) for marking, assessment and reporting purposes. What *has* changed is that students can choose their individual pathway to complete their RATs, one that provides them with choices and takes advantage of their preferred learning styles.

Individual Learning Plans should be made available to students who are underachieving for a variety of reasons and to those students who have not responded well to other forms of differentiation. The only group of students that Individual Learning Plans may not cater to could be highly interpersonal students who may prefer to complete their RATs by working with other students.

References

Jenkins, JR & O'Connor R 2002, 'Early identification and intervention for young children with reading/learning disabilities', in R Bradley, L Danielson & DP Hallahan, eds, *Identification of learning disabilities: Research to practice,* Erlbaum, Mahwah, NJ.

Pirozzo, R 1982, 'Gifted underachievers', *Roeper Review,* vol. 4, no. 4, pp. 18–21.

Queensland Studies Authority 2007, *Learning Difficulties,* Brisbane, Australia.

Westwood, P 2008, *What teachers need to know about learning difficulties,* ACER Press: Melbourne, Victoria.

Chapter 7
Concluding remarks and summary

In researching, compiling and writing this book, we have discovered the importance of recognising the different abilities, learning styles, backgrounds, prior knowledge, interests, experiences and readiness to learn of students in mixed-ability classrooms.. To be successful in differentiating the curriculum, teachers will need to have a great deal of patience, caring, understanding and trust in their students to choose their own individual pathway to success. Two additional key elements teachers need are:

- an in-depth knowledge of their students' reading, mathematics, thinking skills, learning styles and interests
- a strong planning framework that enables them to engage their students through a combination of explicit teaching and choices

To achieve the first item, we have shown how useful the 'Gathering Information for Differentiation' form is for teachers to gather formal and informal information about their students.

To achieve the second item, we have shown how valuable the matrix is in enabling teachers to reconstruct units for differentiation. This strong planning framework derives its strength from Bloom's Taxonomy and its flexibility from Multiple Intelligence Theory. More recently, the work of McTighe and Wiggins (Backward Mapping), Bruner (Spiral Curriculum), Glasser (Choice Theory) and Vygotsky (The Zone of Proximal Development) have been fashioned on the matrix in order to make it responsive to students' learning.

The reading and maths data provided in this book and the results of multiple-intelligence testing confirms that teachers will encounter a huge range of abilities and learning styles in their mixed-ability classrooms. Given this range, 'teaching to the middle' will disadvantage both students with learning difficulties, EAL/D students and disadvantaged learners, and gifted and talented children. Fundamentally, teaching to the middle has been shown to be inappropriate in the multi-age classroom. Where is the middle in a Year 3–5 classroom – does the teacher aim their teaching at a Year 4 level? In this classroom there actually is no middle.

In order to provide for this wide range of abilities and learning styles, previous models have emphasised that teachers can differentiate the curriculum by altering the content, process, products and learning environment. In addition to altering these elements, teachers need to implement a variety of effective learning and teaching strategies in order to fully differentiate the curriculum.

While teachers may not always be able to change the content prescribed by their employing authorities, they have an enormous control in the way they present or package this content for their students. They can choose from six different learning and teaching strategies to deliver this content, as indicated in the Pirozzo Model:

- Ability Grouping
- Cooperative Learning Teams
- Learning Contracts
- Learning Centres,
- Multi-age Grouping
- Individual Learning Plans.

This model relies heavily on teachers' willingness to adopt a multi-level delivery system in order to maximise every students' learning potential. By using these learning and teaching strategies, teachers will provide their students with many exciting pathways that can be used to complete the required Real Assessment Tasks (RATs). These are the culminating products that students will hand in at the completion of the units for marking, assessment and reporting purposes. RATs require students to solve real-world problems, and provide classroom learning that is relevant to the 'real world'.

Rather than just pointing out the challenges faced by teachers in mixed-ability classes, the aim of this book is to show how the six learning and teaching strategies can be implemented.

Ability Grouping

Ability Grouping enables teachers to group their students based on their academic abilities. In using Ability Grouping to deliver the Year 5 geography unit 'Countries of the World', we found that the amount of on-task behaviour improved significantly. This enabled the teacher to concentrate on helping students with their learning, rather than devoting time to 'putting out little fires'. The success of this unit was further confirmed by the fact that the students received more As, Bs and Cs than when the teacher used a more traditional teaching mode.

While opposing tracking or streaming, we favour grouping students heterogeneously for most of the school day, but regroup them according to ability for one of two subjects. Ability Groups may be set up within a class for a specific amount of time to help students who are having difficulty with specific skills or to extend gifted students. Ability Grouping was discovered to be a most appropriate strategy for average learners and bright children.

We discovered that Ability Grouping works well for students with learning difficulties as long as the teacher can rely on some in-class support from teacher assistants, learning enrichment teachers, parents or other teaching and non-teaching personnel. However, if this support is not available, the teacher will be stretched to properly support these students. In these circumstances, we believe that Ability Grouping may not be a suitable learning and teaching strategy for students with learning difficulties, EAL/D and disadvantaged learners.

Cooperative Learning Teams

For those teachers who oppose Ability Grouping on philosophical grounds, Cooperative Learning Teams is an excellent alternative that can be used to differentiate the curriculum. Students are grouped based on their preferred learning styles, rather than academic ability. Students work cooperatively in small teams to complete common tasks, which are structured to maximise student learning, and the learning potential of each team member.

Cooperative Learning Teams rely heavily on positive interdependence and individual accountability. All group members support each other while the individuals pledge to support the group. However, not all students were born with the skills to work cooperatively. If we do not equip our students with these skills, cooperative groups can become very noisy and unproductive. To ensure cooperative learning becomes extremely productive with an acceptable noise level, we recommend a three-pronged approach:

1. Adopt Tuckman's (1965; 1997) five-stage model which shows how teams progress, the behaviours needed to carry out the assigned tasks and how to develop positive interpersonal interactions.

2. Teach students the skills to work well cooperatively.

3. Teach students how to give effective feedback.

By implementing the Year 6 unit, 'Build a Space Station in Outer Space', we found the incidence of discipline issues was extremely low. The level of creativity, willingness to attend school, enjoyment, motivation and self-esteem levels for most students increased greatly.

Cooperative Learning Teams should not be used to provide for the needs of competitive, intrapersonal, bright children.

Learning Contracts

A Learning Contract is a written agreement between a student and a teacher. It enables students to choose the activities they would like to complete and to produce evidence that these activities have been successfully completed in order to receive a certain level of achievement. One of the major aims of Learning Contracts is to encourage students to take responsibility for their own learning, thus becoming less dependent on the teacher. Becoming an active, responsible and self-directed learner is the cornerstone of Learning Contracts and providing students with choices is most important to its success.

To ensure the success of Learning Contracts, we believe that teachers should implement the following four steps:

1. Use the matrix to set up the Learning Contract

2. Devise an appropriate point system

3. Use rubrics for assessment and reporting purposes

4. Track your students' progress

In implementing the Learning Contract 'Why Learn about Plants' for a Year 7 class, we discovered that students showed significant improvement in overall academic performance, working independently, depth and breadth of learning, self-esteem and confidence, intrinsic motivation, critical and creative thinking and problem-solving skills. Other educators have also reported similar findings.

Learning Contracts provide students with structure, while simultaneously giving them the freedom to choose the activities they are interested in. Choices provide students with a great deal of control over their own learning.

We recommend implementing Learning Contracts to maximise the learning potential of gifted and talented students, very competitive learners and boys. They are unlikely to be appropriate for students with learning difficulties, EAL/D learners and disadvantaged students, unless the teacher can rely on some in-class support.

Learning Centres

Learning Centres are based on Multiple Intelligence Theory, and offer teachers the opportunity to have eight different Learning Centres operating simultaneously in their classrooms. We suggest gradually implementing Learning Centres into a classroom. The way Learning Centres are set up greatly depends on the year level, subject area, amount of space available, number of computers and the students' individual learning styles.

The first Learning Centre included this book was developed by teachers Pip Riordan and Ros Mangold to cater to 40 Foundation-level students, based on the story of *The Very Hungry Caterpillar*. Pip and Ros reported that students were highly motivated and eager to achieve their personal best during this unit.

The second Learning Centre was implemented while I was working with thirty Year 9 Science students to complete the unit called 'Marketing Your Boat'. These students also enjoyed working in the Learning Centres. The amount of on-task behaviour improved significantly and often new and unique work was produced.

We discovered that the activities in the original unit could be easily reconstructed to create eight Learning Centres. If teachers wanted to improve academic results, encourage independent learning and develop highly motivated students, Learning Centres are a very effective learning and teaching strategy. Issues may involve the amount of time required in finding materials needed, the lack of space in some classrooms, the noise that may be produced and the few students (often intrapersonal or autistic) who may struggle to concentrate on their work.

Multi-age Grouping

In our review of the related literature, we found that today's age-stratified schooling system is the product of the industrial revolution that began in the 1840s. This led to an unprecedented number of new industries and as more workers were needed, millions of people moved into bigger cities. This population growth, plus the improved transportation system, facilitated the development of large comprehensive schools where the graded education system became the only system.

Multi-age Grouping is designed to increase the heterogeneity of the group, thereby capitalising on the different experiences, knowledge and abilities of children. This represents a major challenge to the current system of grouping students by age.

In forming the ideal multi-age classroom, children of different ages, abilities and gender should be placed in the same classroom with the same teacher for a minimum of three years. Each age group should be randomly selected to ensure a balance of age, gender and ability.

The ideal version of a multi-age classroom will be impossible to implement in small and rural schools where the number of enrolments in each year level is rather small. Multi-age teaching will always exist in small and rural schools where there aren't enough students to create single graded classes. In these schools, teachers are unable to create the ideal multi-age classroom, however they can create hybrid multi-age classes, where some parts of the ideal model are utilised for pedagogical reasons and because the enrolment numbers are too small to form single straight-age classes.

In completing the 'Keeping Healthy' unit, we implemented the hybrid Multi-age Grouping strategy in a Year 3–5 rural classroom. This led to a very positive change in children's behaviour, engagement, commitment and the quality of work produced. Multi-age Grouping has been found to engender feelings of belonging, emotional growth and nurturing.

The hybrid model of the multi-age classroom is an outstanding learning and teaching strategy that should be implemented in small and rural schools for logistical and pedagogical reasons. Having said this, very bright children and highly intrapersonal students are often not suited to this type of learning. Their learning needs can be better met by Ability Grouping, Learning Contracts and Individual Learning Plans.

Individual Learning Plans

An Individual Learning Plan is a written curriculum document that allows a student to select the most appropriate pathway to complete the RATs within a specified amount of time. This learning plan takes advantage of the student's preferred learning styles in order to maximise their learning potential. This should be constructed by the teacher in cooperation with the student and other teaching and non-teaching personnel.

We have shown that units based on the matrix can easily be re-constructed to generate Individual Learning Plans for:

- students with learning difficulties, EAL/D students and disadvantaged children
- average students
- gifted and talented students
- students with significant behavioural issues

We concentrated our efforts on creating Individual Learning Plans for four students: Jeff, Melissa, Cheryl and Pat. These students are of similar age, attend the same school, study the same units and are being taught by the same teacher. In terms of ability, learning styles, interests, aspirations, family backgrounds and behavioural issues, these four students are miles apart. Yet somehow the teacher has to find a way to maximise the learning potential of these four students, as well as the other 26 students in this class.

Traditionally, an Individual Learning Plan could have taken anywhere from 10–15 hours to complete. Here, the matrix becomes extremely useful as it enabled the teacher to reconstruct the existing unit 'Marketing Your Boat'. The teacher was then able to create an Individual Learning Plan for Jeff, Melissa, Cheryl and Pat in less than one hour per student.

In completing these Individual Learning Plans, the students are still expected to complete the RATs for marking, assessment and reporting purposes. Students can choose their individual pathway to complete their RATs, and experience dictates that students will always choose the activities they believe they will be successful at.

Individual Learning Plans should be made available to students who are underachieving for a variety of reasons, and to those students who have not responded well to other forms of differentiation. The one exception is highly interpersonal students, as they may prefer to complete their RATs by working with other students.

Chapter 7 - Concluding Remarks and Summary

Summary

Below is a summary of the strengths and weaknesses relating to the six effective learning and teaching strategies that have been discussed in this book.

Given that every student and teacher is different, this summary should be seen as a guide only, and the comments do not apply to every individual student or teacher.

Summary of Learning and Teaching Strategies

	Ability Groups	Cooperative Learning Teams	Learning Contracts	Learning Centres	Multi-age Grouping	Individual Learning Plans
Students with learning difficulties, EAL/D and disadvantaged students	No, unless they have a good deal of in-class support from teacher assistants, learning enrichment teachers and others	Yes	No, unless they have a good deal of in-class support from teacher assistants, learning enrichment teachers and others	Yes	Yes	Yes
Average students	Yes	Yes	Yes	Yes	Yes	Yes
Gifted and talented students	Yes	No	Yes	Yes	No	Yes
Highly interpersonal students	No	Yes	No	Yes	Yes	No
Highly intrapersonal sstudents	Yes	No	Yes	No	No	Yes

Figure 46

We started this book with the idea that for differentiation to take place, teachers would need an in-depth knowledge of their students' reading and maths abilities, thinking skills, learning styles and interests, and a strong planning framework that enables them to engage their students through a combination of explicit teaching and choices. While we found this to be true, we also discovered that teachers need much more than this if they are to use differentiation effectively. The Pirozzo Model is the umbrella for the six learning and teaching strategies to sit under, serving as a reminder to teachers that Ability Grouping, Cooperative Learning Teams, Learning Centres, Learning Contracts, Multi-age Grouping and Individual Learning Plans do not work independently of each other. Quite the opposite — they should be seen as a mosaic of opportunities, complementing one another.

In our search for the best way to differentiate the curriculum, we did not find one single magic bullet, rather, six bullets, all of them working together to provide teachers with the best opportunity to differentiate the curriculum.

In future, we anticipate that teachers will be highly proactive, having these six learning and teaching strategies available at all times in their classroom so that students, with guidance, will be able to choose the one that suits them the most. This means that we may see some students completing the activities in their Ability Groups, others will be involved with their Cooperative Learning Teams, others will be completing their Learning Contracts, others will be working through a variety of Learning Centres, others will be involved with their Multi-age Groups while other students will be completing their Individual Learning Plans. By doing this, teachers will acknowledge, foster, promote and nurture the individual learning needs of every students in their classroom.

Finally, we conclude with a reminder that without giving students choices, differentiation cannot occur. In other words, no choices — no differentiation!

Appendix 1

An in-depth explanation of the thinking tools mentioned throughout this book is provided in *The Thinking School: Implementing Thinking Skills Across the School* (Pirozzo 2013). Below is a list of these tools, and the page numbers in which in they appear in *The Thinking School*.

A & R (Action and Reaction)	6
ARC (Action, Reaction, Consequences)	6
BROW (Brainstorm, Review, Organise, Write)	11–12
BROWSE (Brainstorm, Review, Organise, Write, Share, Evaluate)	13
Concept maps	14–17
GLOW (Gather, List, Organise, Write)	20–21
ISACS (Identify, Share, Argue, Compromise, Solve)	22–24
ITPE (Identify, Think, Pair, Explain)	25–27
IW5 (Why, Why, Who, What, What)	28–29
LDC (Like, Dislike, Challenges, Changes)	30–31
LEADER (Listen, Explain, Argue, Debate, Elaborate, Reflect)	32–38
LEAP (Listen, Enjoy, Analyse & Arrange, Perform)	39–41
LIMACE (Locate, Identify, Make, Analyse, Compare and Contrast, Evaluate)	42–43
LITE (Like, Improvements, Timeline, Evaluation)	44–45
MACE (Make, Analyse, Compare and Contrast, Evaluate)	46–48
PSDR (Predict, Share, Do, Reflect)	49–50
RedMast (Read, Estimate, Draw, Make, Arrange, Simplify, Think)	51–54
RIB–TT (Ralph's Inquiry–Based Thinking Tool)	55–58
SCRAM (Substitute, Combine, Rate, Act, Modify)	59–62
SCREAM (Separate, Classify, Rate, Explain, Act, Magnify)	63
SOWC Analysis (Strengths, Opportunities, Weaknesses, Consequences)	64–67
STIESA (Show, Think, Imitate, Explore, Sound, Apply)	68–71
TAP (Think All Possibilities)	72–73
TEAM (Think, Explain, Arrange, Make)	74–76
The Rake	77–79
Thinking clouds	80–81
TREC (Think, Read, Estimate, Calculate)	82–84
Venn diagram	85–87
WASPS (Watch, Ask, Show, Practise, Show)	88–93
WINCE (Want, Identify, Need, Create, Evaluate)	94–95
W chart	96–98
X chart	99–100
Y chart	101–102
TPS and TPSS	106–109

Appendix 2

Activity 23: Why do some objects float and other sink?

For this activity, you will need:
- a large bowl (either clear plastic or glass)
- the following fruits and vegetables:

  - Apples
  - Bananas
  - Carrots
  - Cucumbers
  - Garlic
  - Grapes
  - Green pepper
  - Kiwi fruit
  - Mandarins
  - Nuts
  - Onions
  - Oranges
  - Potatoes
  - Pumpkins
  - Tomatoes
  - Zucchini
- PSDR method
- TAP technique

Learning activities

- Use the PSDR method to predict what will happen when these fruits and vegetables are placed in water.

- Which of the fruits and vegetables float and which sink?

- Can you explain why some fruits and vegetables float whereas others sink?

- Was the PSDR method of any value to you?

- Let us suppose that when a potato is placed in water it sinks quickly to the bottom. What can you do to make it float? (You cannot use any weights and/or strings). Brainstorm all possibilities by using TAP.

- Now, try your experiment. Does it work?

- Reflect on the outcome of your experiment. If for some reason your experiment did not work, what can you do differently?

www.ingramcontent.com/pod-product-compliance
Lightning Source LLC
Chambersburg PA
CBHW081918090526
44590CB00019B/3391